Advanced
Adobe Photoshop™

Library of Congress Catalog No.: 94-76913 (Windows platform) 94-76912 (Macintosh platform)

ISBN: 1-56830-116-2 (Windows platform) 1-56830-117-0 (Macintosh platform)

10 9 8 7 6 5 4 3 2

The information in this book is furnished for informational use only, is subject to change without notice, and should not be construed as a commitment by Adobe Systems Incorporated. Adobe Systems Incorporated assumes no responsibility for any errors or inaccuracies that may appear in this book. The software and typefaces mentioned in this book are furnished under license and may only be used or copied in accordance with the terms of such license.

PANTONE®* Computer video simulations used in this product may not match PANTONE-identified solid color standards. Use current PANTONE Color Reference Manuals for accurate color. *Pantone, Inc.'s check-standard trademark for color. PANTONE Color Computer Graphics" © Pantone, Inc. 1986, 1993.

Pantone, Inc. is the copyright owner of PANTONE Color Computer Graphics and Software which are licensed to Adobe to distribute for use only in combinations with Adobe Photoshop. PANTONE Color Computer Graphics and Software shall not be copied onto another diskette or into memory unless as part of the execution of Adobe Photoshop.

PostScript™ is a trademark of Adobe Systems Incorporated ("Adobe"), registered in the United States and elsewhere. PostScript can refer both to the PostScript language as specified by Adobe and to Adobe's implementation of its PostScript language interpreter.

Any references to "PostScript printers," "PostScript files," or "PostScript printer drivers" refer, respectively, to printers, files and driver programs written in or supporting the PostScript language. References in this book to the "PostScript language" are intended to emphasize Adobe's standard definition of that language.

Printed in the United States of America by Shepard Poorman Communications, Indianapolis, Indiana.

Published simultaneously in Canada.

Adobe Press™ books are published and distributed by Hayden Books, a division of Macmillan Computer Publishing, USA. For individual orders, or for educational, corporate, or retail sales accounts, call 1-800-428-5331. For information address Macmillan Computer Publishing, 201 West 103 Street, Indianapolis, IN 46290.

Contents

By manipulating layers to show and hide various colors and fonts, it is possible to offer your clients countless variations of an image within a single document. Creating this packaging presentation includes using the pen tool to draw a curved path and a straight-line path, creating a clipping group, and making a selection using the Color Range command.

Using the Apply Image command to copy images from one file to another without adding a layer helps to reduce the demand for disk space on your system. This project also features using Quick Mask mode to make a selection.

After editing a layer mask with the gradient tool, you will export the image to Adobe Illustrator,™ place type on a curved path in Adobe Illustrator, and then import the type into Adobe Photoshop. Once you finish assembling the image, you will convert the document from Grayscale mode to Duotone mode in order to apply a green tint.

In addition to creating layer masks, this project features tips and techniques for creative manipulation of images that include darkening an image with the burn tool and producing geometrical distortions of selections.

Following a recommended approach for controlling the color of an image, you will use the Adobe Photoshop program's powerful new color correction tools that include the Gamut Warning command, the CMYK Preview command, the Replace Color command, and the Selective Color command.

This project features making the most of the new layering feature in the Adobe Photoshop program to create three multimedia display screens that can be stored in a single document.

Designers, illustrators, photographers, prepress professionals , and video and multimedia artists use Adobe Photoshop™ software, the world's leading desktop image design and production tool, to create original artwork, correct color, retouch and

WHY AN ADVANCED BOOK?

composite scanned images, and prepare professional-quality separations and output with more flexibility that ever before.

With a new layering feature, Adobe Photoshop 3.0 makes it possible to draw, edit, and paste on separate layers. Layers, like transparent sheets of acetate, allow you to try out different combinations of images or placements of graphics, text, and special effects, and then change your mind and simply lift them out.

Classroom in a Book: Advanced Adobe Photoshop™ introduces an advanced approach to using layers. In addition to the new layering feature, this book covers advanced tips and techniques for using the new tools and features, such as the new palette design, the new color controlling tools, and the new ways to apply special effects. Use *Advanced Adobe Photoshop* to discover a more convenient way of working with Adobe Photoshop, giving you stronger creative control and improved production capabilities.

ADVANCED PREREQUISITES

Advanced Adobe Photoshop is designed for users who are familiar with Adobe Photoshop. Since this book shows you advanced techniques for using Adobe Photoshop, the instructional material assumes you know the application, your computer, and general graphic arts terminology.

If you're new to Adobe Photoshop, begin with the second edition of *Classroom in a Book: Adobe Photoshop™*, and then proceed to this book, *Advanced Adobe Photoshop*. You can order these books by calling the publisher 1-800-428-5331.

SELF-PACED LEARNING FOR BUSY USERS

Developed and tested at Adobe Systems, Inc., each book in the *Classroom in a Book* series features a collection of design projects. Each project consists of step-by-step instructions for composing and editing an image. Not only do you set the pace, it's up to you when and where you do the work.

CROSS-PLATFORM COMPATIBILITY

Adobe Photoshop features the same interface across the Macintosh®, Windows™, and UNIX® platforms. For this reason, this book was developed to be used on any platform. Once you learn Adobe Photoshop on one platform, you'll find it easy to use on another. The following dialog boxes illustrate just how similar Adobe Photoshop is across platforms.

Macintosh   *Windows*

Rather than illustrating this book with dialog boxes from a specific platform, or alternating between the three platforms, we altered the appearance of Macintosh dialog boxes to create dialog boxes that apply to all platforms. The dialog box shown below illustrates the cross-platform version of the dialog boxes shown above.

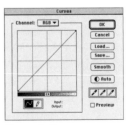

Cross-platform

In addition, the cross-platform compatibility of Adobe Photoshop makes it possible to open and edit the same file on all platforms. As a result, the *Advanced Adobe Photoshop* CD-ROM disc provides a single set of files to be used with any platform.

UNIX platform: *Use the keyboard equivalents chart shown below to map either Macintosh or Windows key sequences described in this book to your keyboard assignments.*

MACINTOSH	WINDOWS	SGI DEFAULT MODIFIER	SUN DEFAULT MODIFIER	SGI NEW MODIFIER	SUN NEW MODIFIER
Shift	Shift	Shift	Shift	Shift	Shift
Command	Control	Control	Control	Alt	Meta
Option	Alt	Alt	Meta	Ctrl_L	Alt
Control	None	None	None	Ctrl_R	Control

A SEMINAR IN A BOOK

This book includes 12 advanced projects. Each project contains step-by-step instructions for creating the image, along with lots of explanations and tips and techniques.

With the fashion industry as the central theme for the book, you will compose and edit images for a variety of fictitious concerns from designers to publishers to clothing manufacturers. Within this context, you'll work on an invitation to a fashion show, a magazine cover, an exhibition poster, a packaging mock-up presentation, and more.

To get you started on the right track, the first project shows you how to calibrate your monitor.

Project 2 gives you an overview of the Adobe Photoshop application's latest features, including palettes and layers, and you will use the layering feature to create several variations of an image in a single document. In Project 3, you will retouch an image using the new Dust & Scratches filter.

Project 4 introduces you to layer masks while you create a magazine advertisement for a fragrance manufacturer. In Project 5, you combine a variety of images to create a striking exhibition poster of African art, and you will create a clipping group. In Project 6, you will have combine a variety of techniques to create a billboard, featuring a spectacular ripple background.

Project 7 features how to use the new layering feature to create numerous variations of a mock-up design in a single Adobe Photoshop document. Then in Project 8 you will put it all together to create the cover of an annual report.

You will compose a grayscale image to be used for a newspaper ad in Project 9, and then you will convert the image to duotone mode. Project 10 features a brochure cover design, with two examples of using the layer mask feature. In Project 11, you color correct an image to be used for a magazine cover. Project 12, the final project, gives you information on using Adobe Photoshop as a multimedia production tool for designing display screens.

Before you start working on an *Advanced Adobe Photoshop* project, make sure that your system is set up correctly and that you have installed the recommended software and hardware. The following listing summarizes what you need to do:

WHAT YOU NEED TO DO

- Check the system requirements and recommendations described in the *Getting Started* booklet that comes with the Adobe Photoshop software.

- Install the Adobe Photoshop application, as described in the *Getting Started* booklet.

- Install the fonts included on the *Advanced Adobe Photoshop* CD-ROM disc.

- Copy the files (included on the *Advanced Adobe Photoshop* CD-ROM disc) to your hard drive.

CHECKING THE SYSTEM REQUIREMENTS AND RECOMMENDATIONS

To access the *Advanced Adobe Photoshop* CD-ROM disc files, you need a double-speed or higher CD-ROM drive.

To execute the projects in *Advanced Adobe Photoshop*, it's best if your system includes the hardware and software recommended in the *Getting Started* booklet that comes with the Adobe Photoshop software. Important here, because these recommendations exceed the system requirements (also discussed in *Getting Started*) for running the Adobe Photoshop application. Although it may be possible to execute these projects without all recommended hardware and software; the more your system approaches these recommendations, the more your success is ensured.

To watch Adobe Teach™ movies, your system must meet or exceed the following requirements:

Macintosh platform:
8 MB of free RAM
System 7.0
256 colors monitor
double-speed or higher CD-ROM drive.
QuickTime™ installed in your system.

Note: To install QuickTime, place the QuickTime extension from the QuickTime 1.6.1 folder in your system folder.

Windows platform:
8 MB of free RAM
486/33 MHz or better CPU
DOS 5.0
Windows 3.1
VGA+ display (256 colors at 640x480 resolution)
sound card
double-speed or higher CD-ROM drive.

UNIX platform: Adobe Teach movies play on the Macintosh platform or the Windows platform only.

INSTALLING ADOBE PHOTOSHOP

This book does not include the Adobe Photoshop software. You must purchase the software separately. Using the *Getting Started* booklet that comes with the Adobe Photoshop software, install the Adobe Photoshop application.

INSTALLING THE FONTS

In addition to using some commonly used fonts, many of the projects included in this book feature Adobe Originals™ fonts. These fonts are found on the *Advanced Adobe Photoshop* CD-ROM disc in the *Fonts* folder (or directory).

Unix platform: Substitute the following fonts with whatever fonts are available on your system.

Install the fonts listed below.

Adobe Garamond™: Projects 6
Birch™: Project 9
Lithos™: Project 5
Madrone™: Projects 7, 10
Minion™: Project 7
Myriad™: Project 7
Viva™: Projects 8, 11
Willow™: Projects 10, 11

COPYING THE *ADVANCED ADOBE PHOTOSHOP* FILES

The *Advanced Adobe Photoshop*™ CD-ROM disc includes files for all projects. The files are locked for your protection, so that you don't inadvertently write over the original files.

Copy the following folders (or directories) to your hard disk to access the files for the projects. To save room, copy the files for each project as needed.

01Project	08Project
02Project	09Project
03Project	10Project
04Project	11Project
05Project	12Project
06Project	Fonts
07Project	HighRes

For the sake of increasing efficiency, we have designed these projects to use low-resolution files. The high-resolution versions of these images that include full rights, are found on the CD-ROM disc in *HighRes*.

Important: *All images in* 02Project *through* 12Project *and in HighRes are copyright free. The* Photo.psd *file in* 01Project *is copyright protected.*

We recommend that you create a folder (or directory) named *Projects*. As you work through the projects in this book, store the files that you create in *Projects*.

WATCHING ADOBE TEACH MOVIES

Adobe Teach movies are QuickTime movies included with *Advanced Adobe Photoshop*. You can watch a movie to see a preview of what's to come in a project, or you can go back and review the movie after you've tried a new technique. You can even watch a movie right now. You'll see the Adobe Teach movie icon whenever it's time to watch a movie.

Depending on the amount of memory you have, you may have to close the Adobe Photoshop application while you watch the movie.

1 Quit (or exit) the Adobe Photoshop application.

2 Open the Adobe Teach movie menu:

Macintosh platform: *Open the* C_I_Book *folder found on the* Advanced Adobe Photoshop *CD-ROM disc, and then double-click the* Classroom In A Book.APS *icon.*

Windows platform: *Double-click* cibook.exe *in the root directory of the Advanced Adobe Photoshop CD-ROM disc.*

The Adobe Teach movie menu prompts you to make a selection.

Note: *If you have any difficultly opening the Adobe Teach movie menu, open the* Data *folder (or directory) in the* C_I_Book *folder (or directory) to play the movies independently with QuickTime.*

3 Click the red movie button to open a movie.

The movie begins playing. To stop, start, or rewind a movie, use the movie controller below the movie window.

Macintosh platform: *To adjust the volume of a movie, press keyboard numbers 1 through 7.*

4 To return to the Adobe Teach movie menu, click the Return button below the movie window.

5 In the Adobe Teach movie menu, select another movie to be played or click the Exit button.

Note: *For information about compatibility issues, refer to the* Read-me *file on the CD-ROM disc.*

READ THE MANUAL

For comprehensive information about all of the application's features, refer to the *Adobe Photoshop User Guide*. You will find the *Quick Reference Card*, packaged with Adobe Photoshop, a useful companion as you work through the lessons in this book. For additional information on advanced techniques, see *Beyond the Basics*, included with the documentation that comes with the Adobe Photoshop software.

1

Before you begin working with Adobe Photoshop, it's a good idea to calibrate your monitor. Since many uncalibrated monitors tend to display a bluish cast, eliminating the cast means the monitor grays will appear as neutral as possible. If you

Monitor Calibration

do not get rid of a color cast you may, for example, add yellow and red to an image to compensate for a blue cast; the result will be a printed image that has a yellow and red color cast. ■ After using the Adobe Photoshop calibration program to fine-tune your monitor, you will enter specifications in the Monitor Setup dialog box. The Monitor Setup dialog box includes options that give Adobe Photoshop information about lighting, viewing, and monitor configurations. This data is then used to create color separations.

Several other factors can affect your final output. For example, the quality of the final output can vary dramatically, with the imagesetter, the strength and the mixture of the chemicals, the batch of film used, the paper stock used, and the

MONITOR CALIBRATION

nature of the press. For this reason, it is important to calibrate your monitor and adjust your settings to compensate for any unusual output conditions.

You can use the Adobe Photoshop calibration tools to ensure that the image on your screen matches your printed output by affecting how images appear on-screen and how Adobe Photoshop converts color from RGB to CMYK mode. To calibrate your entire system, refer to the step-by-step instructions in the *Adobe Photoshop User Guide*.

USING THE ADOBE PHOTOSHOP MONITOR CALIBRATION PROGRAM

With the grayscale image open, you can observe how your adjustments affect the shadows, highlights, and midtones of the image.

In addition to opening a grayscale image, you will open a file that displays a field of solid medium gray, providing a clear view of the effects of your adjustments to the color cast of the gray field.

Note: *Third party monitor calibration systems provide another means to calibrate your monitors.*

Standardizing your work environment

The first adjustment you'll make is to standardize your room lighting and monitor settings so that the calibration will be accurate for your work environment.

1 Make sure your monitor has been turned on for at least a half hour so that the monitor display has been stabilized.

2 Set the room lighting at the level you plan to maintain, then adjust the brightness and contrast controls on your monitor.

Because changes in lighting, brightness, and contrast can dramatically affect your display, try to keep the room free from external light sources. Tape down your brightness and contrast controls once you've set them.

Calibrating your monitor

After throwing away the Adobe Photoshop preferences file, you will calibrate your monitor by setting a target gamma, then adjusting the whites, the color balance, the blacks, and finally the grays (gamma).

1 Before you launch the Adobe Photoshop application, throw away the Adobe Photoshop preferences file to ensure all settings are returned to their default values.

Macintosh platform: *Drag the* Adobe Photoshop 3.0 Prefs *file in the* Preferences *folder (in the* System *folder) to the Trash icon.*

Windows platform: *Delete the* Photos30.psp *file in the* Windows *directory.*

UNIX platform: *Delete the Adobe* %Photoshop Prefs *file and the Adobe* Photoshop Prefs *file in the* <workingdir>/Photoshop.MacFiles/System/Preferences *directory.*

2 Launch the Adobe Photoshop application, and open the files *Photo.psd* and *Gray.psd* in *01Project*.

3 Start the calibration program.

Macintosh platform: *Choose Control Panels from the Apple menu, and in the Control Panels dialog box double-click* Gamma, *close the Control Panel dialog box, in the Gamma Control Panel make sure the On button is selected, and make sure a target gamma of 1.8 is selected.*

Windows and UNIX platforms: *Choose Preferences from the File menu and Monitor Setup from the submenu, and in the Monitor Setup dialog box make sure the target gamma is set to 1.8 in the Gamma box, click the Calibrate option to open the Calibrate dialog box.*

A target gamma of 1.8 is recommended for printing CMYK images. If you are sending your output to an RGB device, use a higher target. Images intended for video should have a target gamma of 2.2, typical for most television sets.

4 Adjust the positioning of the *Photo.psd* document and the *Gray.psd* document on your desktop to make them as viewable as possible.

Before calibrating the color balance, and white and black points of color and the grayscale monitors, you will adjust the gamma.

5 Drag the triangle on the Gamma Adjustment slider left and right until the gamma strip above the slider appears to be solid gray without any striping.

6 With the White Pt option selected, hold up a white piece of paper in a color of the stock on which you will be printing and drag the Red, Green, and Blue slider triangles until the monitor white matches the paper as closely as possible.

For maximum accuracy, view the paper under controlled lighting, such as a light box or a combination fluorescent and tungsten light bulb.

If your terminal displays light with a bluish tint, you may want the highlights to appear in warmer tones. With the triangles forming an even slope as shown in the illustration below, set this slope as steep or as gradual to best suit your needs.

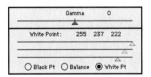

Note: *If your terminal displays light with a reddish tint, it may be suitable to arrange the White point sliders with the reverse slope.*

7 With the Balance option selected, drag the Red, Green, and Blue slider triangles until the monitor grays (in the *Gray.psd* document or the gamma strip) appear to be neutral.

The Balance option controls the monitor's mixture of red, green, and blue, and compensates for color casts in the monitor.

Note: It may be helpful to match the gray midtone to a Kodak™ gray card (as you did with the paper stock) to achieve more accurate results.

8 With the Black Pt option selected, drag the three slider triangles to the right until you can see a distinct gradation between each swatch in the strip below the sliders, vertically aligning the Red, Green, and Blue sliders to prevent color tint appearing in the shadow tones as shown in the illustration below.

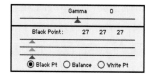

9 If necessary, readjust color balance and the gamma, and click OK.

Windows and UNIX platforms: *Since your calibration settings are discarded whenever you throw away the Adobe Photoshop preferences files, click the Save button to make it possible to load these calibration settings later.*

Macintosh platform: *Close the Gamma Control Panel and the Control panel window.*

If you are using more than one monitor, the monitor calibration program provides the ability to maintain the calibration settings for two active monitors. It is also possible to save and load custom gamma settings for different paper stocks and for different monitors.

Note: The monitor calibration program only affects the monitor display. In Windows and Unix platforms, the monitor calibration program affects only the monitor display when you are using the Adobe Photoshop application.

USING THE MONITOR SETUP DIALOG BOX

Now that you have calibrated your monitor, you will enter monitor specifications in the Monitor Setup dialog box.

Adobe Photoshop uses the information in the Monitor Setup dialog box to compensate for factors affecting the monitor display such as the target gamma and white point, the type of phosphors in the monitor, and the room lighting conditions. In addition to affecting overall monitor display, the Monitor Setup information determines how the program converts colors between RGB and CMYK modes and how the overall brightness of images is displayed.

1 To enter Monitor Setup information, make sure the Adobe Photoshop application is active, and choose Preferences from the File menu and Monitor Setup from the submenu.

2 In the Monitor Setup dialog box choose the monitor you are using from the Monitor pop-up menu.

3 Make sure 6500K (the default value) is specified in the White Point pop-up menu.

Note: If you are using a third-party monitor calibration device, choose the value established by that device; otherwise, if the value you need is not in the list, select Custom and type in your own values.

4 Choose the monitor type from the Phosphors pop-up menu.

Note: If the correct type is not in the pop-up menu, choose Custom and enter the red, green, and blue chromaticity coordinates as specified by your monitor manufacturer. This option compensates for the different red, green, and blue phosphors used by monitors to display color.

5 Choose one of the following settings from the Ambient Light pop-up menu:

• Select High if your room lighting is brighter than the image on-screen.

• Select Low if it is not as bright as the screen.

• Select Medium if the light levels are about the same.

6 Click OK to close the dialog box.

7 Close the *Photo.psd* and *Gray.psd* files, leaving the Adobe Photoshop application open.

Also, it is best if you calibrate your monitors periodically since the way a monitor displays images varies over time. How often you recalibrate depends mostly on how quickly a monitor deviates from its calibration. In general, as a monitor ages, more frequent recalibration is needed.

2

Using a photographic image as the central element for this project, you will create several variations (within a single document) of what will be an invitation to a Moscow reception

INVITATION COVER DESIGN

where the latest fashions in footwear will be shown. The photograph, shot on a white background and cast in deep yellow light, features an antique Italian shoe form resting on jars of caviar. ■ Before you begin creating the invitation, this project offers you a chance to become familiar with Adobe Photoshop 3.0. After opening a final version of the invitation, you can follow the step-by-step instructions to get acquainted with the new layering feature and the user interface.

The central photographic image was scanned on a Leafscan 45 transparency scanner from a 2¼ inch photo transparency with a scan resolution of 300 dpi (dots per inch) and saved as TIFF file format, an Adobe Photoshop-compatible file format.

INVITATION COVER DESIGN

For the sake of reducing the demand for disk space on your system, you will create the invitation using a working file with a 72 ppi resolution. The original high resolution file is available on the *Advanced Adobe Photoshop*™ CD-ROM disc.

In addition to introducing you to the new layering feature, this project focuses attention on how to use the layering feature to experiment with countless effects in a single document.

This project covers:

• Using the Preserve Transparency option

• Copying layers and selections from one file to another

• Saving a selection to a channel mask

• Applying the Emboss filter

• Drawing with the line tool

• Displaying the file size, dimensions and resolution of the document

• Selecting an interpolation method

• Merging layers

• Rotating an image

• Defining a pattern

• Setting a layer to Difference mode

• Applying the Ripple filter.

It should take you about 2½ hours to complete this project.

Viewing the final image

Take this moment to look at the invitation that you will create.

1 In the Adobe Photoshop application, open the *02Final.psd* file in *02Project* to view the final image.

THE PALETTES

By default, the document window displays the toolbox and eight of the ten Adobe Photoshop palettes in three groups. Two remaining palettes (the Info palette and the Command palette) are hidden and when opened, are displayed independently.

Displaying the palettes

To display a specific palette, you can choose the appropriate Show command in the Window menu or click a palette tab to make it the front most palette in a group.

1 Choose Palettes from the Window menu and Show Info from the submenu to open the Info palette.

TIP: TO COLLAPSE OR
EXPAND A PALETTE,
DOUBLE-CLICK THE
PALETTE TAB. TO COL-
LAPSE PALETTE GROUP
TO THE PALETTE TITLE
ONLY (WITHOUT THE
SUBMENUS), HOLD
DOWN THE OPTION
KEY (OR THE ALT
KEY) AND CLICK
THE ZOOM BOX.

Note: *Leaving the Info palette open at all times makes it possible to view information about the selected tool and the color values beneath the cursor.*

2 Choose Palettes from the Window menu and Show Commands from the submenu to open the Commands palette.

Note: *When you are working with a keyboard that has function keys, you can use the Commands palette to choose frequently used commands. You can change the preassigned commands and assign function keys to additional commands.*

3 Choose Palettes from the Window menu and Show Swatches from the submenu to make the Swatches palette appear in the front of the Picker/Swatches/Scratch group.

Note: *The Picker/Swatches/Scratch group contains the options to choose, edit, and create colors.*

4 Click the Picker tab to make it appear at the front of the Picker/Swatches/Scratch group.

5 Double-click the paintbrush tool in the toolbox to open the corresponding Paintbrush Options palette, making it the front most palette in the Brushes/Options group.

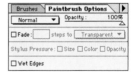

Note: *The Brushes/Options group contains the options you need for painting and editing.*

6 Press the Tab key to hide all open palettes, including the toolbox.

7 Press the Tab key to display all open palettes, including the toolbox.

Organizing the palettes

It is probably most convenient to leave the palettes open while you work.

1 To better organize your palettes, drag the Commands palette and the Info palette to the upper-right corner of the desktop, and make sure the three palette groups are positioned at the bottom of your desktop as shown in the illustration below, taking advantage of the snap-to-edge function that is built into each palette.

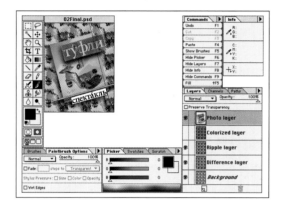

It is possible to group or ungroup any of the ten palettes to best suit your needs.

2 To customize the palette groupings, drag the Brushes palette tab to the Picker/Swatches/Scratch group.

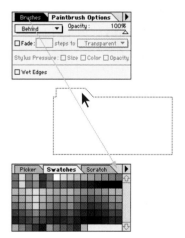

TIP: TO VIEW A LAYER, HIDING ALL OTHER LAYERS, CLICK NEAR THE LAYER NAME (TO THE RIGHT OF THE LAYER ICON) IN THE LAYERS PALETTE, WHICH ALSO SELECTS THE LAYER.

The Paintbrush Options palette appears as an independent palette.

3 Drag to return the Brushes palette to the Paintbrush Options palette to return the palettes to the default groupings.

4 To increase your workspace, collapse all palette groups by clicking the zoom box in the right-most corner of the title bar.

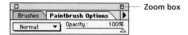
— Zoom box

The submenus in the palettes are displayed even when the palette is collapsed.

5 Click the zoom box in the right-most corner of the Layers palette title bar to expand the Layers palette.

THE LAYERS PALETTE

The Layers palette displays the five layers used to create this document, starting with the front most layer, Photo layer. Since the Photo layer is the selected layer, the Layers palette also displays its selected mode and opacity. The Background layer, always the bottom-most layer, is created as part of every new document.

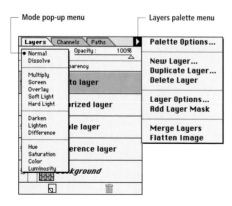
Mode pop-up menu — Layers palette menu

The layers that you create act as transparent acetate sheets. By drawing, editing, and pasting on separate layers, you can try out different combinations and placements of type, graphics, and special effects, without altering the Background layer.

Time out for a movie

If your system is capable of running Adobe Teach movies, you can see an introduction to the new layering feature. Play the movie named Layers Palette. For information on how to play Adobe Teach movies, see the "What You Need To Do" section at the beginning of this book.

Showing and hiding layers

You can click on the eye icon in the left-most column of a layer in the Layers palette to show or hide a layer in the document window.

1 Click the eye icon in the left-most column of the Photo layer in the Layers palette to hide the Photo layer in the document window.

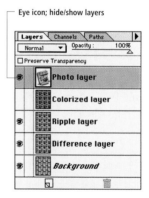
Eye icon; hide/show layers

2 Click the eye icon in the left-most column of the Ripple layer in the Layers palette to hide the Ripple layer in the document window.

TIP: DRAG A FLOAT-
ING SELECTION TO
THE TRASH ICON IN
THE LOWER-RIGHT
CORNER OF THE
LAYERS PALETTE
TO DELETE IT.

The background pattern of the Difference layer is now visible in the document window.

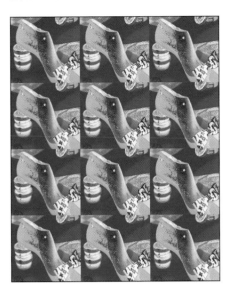

3 Drag through the entire left column in the Layers palette to show all layers.

Note: To hide multiple layers, drag through the left column in the Layers palette.

4 To view the Photo layer in the document window, hiding all other layers, hold down the Option key (or the Alt key) and click the left-most column of the Photo layer in the Layers palette.

With only the Photo layer displayed in the document window, it is possible to view the checkerboard pattern, representing the transparent areas of the layer. The checkerboard pattern helps you to distinguish between transparent areas and opaque areas of a layer.

5 Hold down the Option key (or the Alt key) and click the eye icon in the Photo layer again to make all layers visible in the document window.

Editing a layer

You can use the painting and editing tools to draw on a layer, or you can copy and paste selections to a layer. All editing takes place on the current target layer and in the current target channel.

Note: Only one layer can be edited at a time. When using the rubber stamp tool or the smudge tool, however, all the visible layers are edited.

1 Click the Background layer in the Layers palette to make it the target layer.

The Background layer is highlighted (and the layer name appears in the document window's title bar). You can edit only one target layer at a time.

Limiting editing on a layer

When you create a new layer in an image, the layers are 100% transparent. Pasting, painting, and editing in the layer fill certain areas with pixels (color values), making them opaque. Once you have added color values to a layer you might wish to confine all further editing to the opaque areas.

For example, you may have created a layer for type, where you want to add special effects to the type, affecting only the type characters.

1 With the Background layer selected in the Layers palette, select the marquee tool, and drag to select one tile from the pattern as shown in the illustration below.

2 Choose Copy from the Edit menu to copy the pattern to the Clipboard.

3 Click the Photo layer in the Layers palette, selecting it to be the target layer, and then click the Preserve Transparency option in the Layers palette.

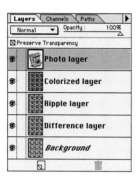

You will paste a selection to the Photo layer, so that you can observe how the pasted selection is applied to a layer that has the Preserve Transparency option activated.

4 With the Photo layer selected in the Layers palette, choose Paste from the Edit menu.

The Layers palette displays a Floating Selection above the current target layer, Photo layer. The selection is floating because it sits on a plane above the target layer. In effect the floating selection is a temporary layer. The pixels don't merge with the underlying layer until you deselect the floating selection.

Note: Selecting another layer deselects a floating selection.

5 With the move tool selected, position the cursor over the floating selection in the document window, and drag so that it overlaps transparent areas of the Photo layer.

Only the opaque areas show the floating selection.

Note: When you use the pencil, paintbrush, airbrush, rubber-stamp, paint bucket, and gradient tools, only the opaque areas of a layer show the effects of the tool for a layer set to Preserve Transparency.

6 With the Floating Selection still highlighted in the Layers palette, press the Delete key to delete the floating selection.

To limit editing on a layer, you would select the target layer in the Layers palette, and click the Preserve Transparency option in the Layers palette.

Displaying layer thumbnails

A layer thumbnail, representing the contents of a layer, appears to the left of the layer name in the Layers palette. So that you can continue editing a layer without waiting for the layer thumbnail to be updated, the layer thumbnail is automatically updated when the processor is idle.

Using a smaller layer thumbnail or turning off the layer thumbnail can improve performance and save disk space.

1 To change the size of the layer thumbnail, choose Palette Options from the Layers palette menu (right triangle) in the Layers palette, in the Palette Layer Options dialog box make sure the smallest layer thumbnail size is selected, and click OK.

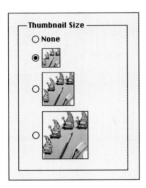

Reordering layers

You can reorder layers (and Floating Selections) by dragging a layer (or a Floating Selection) up or down in the Layers palette.

Note: *The Background layer cannot be moved and is always the bottom layer in a document. To move the Background layer to a different position in the stack of layers, use the Duplicate Layer command to make a copy of the Background layer and move the copy in the Layers palette. Delete the original Background layer.*

1 In the Layers palette drag the Photo layer below the Colorized layer.

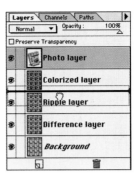

The Photo layer is now completely obscured in the document window by the Colorized layer.

2 In the Layers palette drag the Photo layer to the top of the layers stack, returning it to its original position.

Moving layers in the Layers palette

Using the move tool, you will move a selected layer independently (without affecting other layers) in any direction in the document window. You can also link multiple layers in the Layers palette and move them together in the document window.

Note: *In addition to moving a layer or linked layers, the move tool is used to move selections in the document window.*

1 With the Photo layer selected in the Layers palette and with the move tool selected in the toolbox, position the cursor over the image in the document window, and drag the Photo layer in any direction in the document window.

Note: Hold down the Shift key as you drag to constrain the movement to 45° or 90°.

2 Press the arrow keys to move the layer in one pixel increments.

Note: Hold down the Shift key as you press the arrow keys to move the layer in 10 pixel increments.

Any areas of the layer that are dragged outside of the window are automatically clipped when you save the document.

Linking layers to be moved in the document window

After linking two layers in the Layers palette, you will move them together in the document window.

1 With the Photo layer selected in the Layers palette, click the second column from the left in the Ripple layer to link it to the Photo layer.

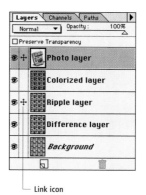

Link icon

The link icons are displayed in the second column from the left for both layers, indicating the layers are linked and can be moved in the document window as one unit.

2 With either Photo layer or Ripple layer selected in the Layers palette and with the move tool still selected, position the cursor over the document window, and drag the linked layers in any direction to move them as one unit in the document window.

You will link a third layer to the Photo layer and the Ripple layer.

3 In the Layers palette click the second column from the left in the Difference layer to link it to the other two layers.

4 Again, with the move tool selected, position the cursor over the document window, and drag the linked layers in any direction to move them as one unit in the document window.

5 In the Layers palette click the link icon of the selected layer to unlink all layers.

6 Choose Revert from the File menu, and when prompted click the Revert button.

TIP: PRESS THE ARROW
KEYS TO MOVE A
SELECTION IN ONE
PIXEL INCREMENTS.

Adding a new layer

You can create any number of layers in a document; however, the amount of memory your system has may affect the number of layers you can have in a single document.

After selecting the Difference layer in the Layers palette, you will add a new layer that will be automatically positioned above the Difference layer.

Note: You can create a layer no matter which channel is your target channel. Once you add a new layer, the composite channel automatically becomes the target channel.

1 With the Difference layer selected in the Layers palette, choose New Layer from the Layers palette menu in the Layers palette.

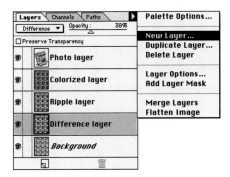

The New Layer dialog box prompts you to name the new layer. In addition to specifying the opacity and mode for the new layer, you can specify whether or not to group it into a clipping group, a topic to be covered in a later project.

2 In the New Layers dialog box type **New layer** in the Name box, and click OK.

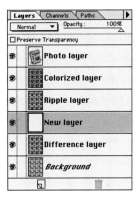

The New layer is placed above the layer (Difference layer) that was selected in the Layers palette.

3 In the Layers palette double-click the New layer, in the Layer Options palette type **New name layer** in the Name box, and click OK.

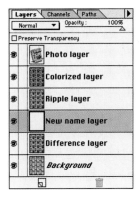

The New name layer is displayed in the Layers palette.

Deleting a layer

1 To delete the New name layer, make sure the New name layer is selected in the Layers palette, and choose Delete Layer from the Layers palette menu in the Layers palette.

2 Revert to the saved copy of the *02Final.psd* file.

3 Make sure all layers are displayed (eye icon visible in the Layers palette).

4 Reduce the view of the *02Final.psd* document, and drag it to the upper-right corner of your desktop for use as a visual reference.

CREATING A DOCUMENT

After opening a new file, you will copy the necessary components of the image from a file containing a library of collected images, applying painting and editing tools and filters to the working file.

Opening a new document

1 Choose New from the File menu, in the New dialog box type **02Work.psd** in the Name box, **360** pixels in the Width box and **442** pixels in the Height box, **72** ppi in the Resolution box, make sure RGB color is selected from the Mode pop-up menu, and click OK.

By default, the Layers palette displays the Background layer, and the document window displays the Background layer's default white background.

Opening the library of images

Rather than moving three images from three separate Adobe Photoshop files, you will copy three images from a single file, *02Lib.psd*, to the *02Work.psd* file.

1 Open the *02Lib.psd* file in *02Project*.

The *02Lib.psd* file is a library of images, consisting of three images on three separate layers. While a library is well suited to organize the components of a project, it is not meant to serve as a working file for composing or processing a composite image.

2 Experiment with hiding and showing various layers.

Placing the photo image

Before creating the repeating pattern on the Background layer, you will place the central photographic image on a layer of its own. Using the Duplicate Layer command, you will copy the Photo layer from the *02Lib.psd* file to the *02Work.psd* file.

Note: *Although dragging the Photo layer (from the Layers palette of the source file to the document window of the target file) copies the entire layer to the target file and automatically adds a new layer to the target file, the Duplicate layer command works best for this example because the image is automatically centered in the work canvas of the target document.*

1 In the Layers palette of the *02Lib.psd* file make sure the Photo layer is selected.

2 In the Layers palette choose Duplicate Layer from the Layers palette menu, in the Duplicate Layer dialog box choose the *02Work.psd* file from the Document pop-up menu in the Destination box, and click OK.

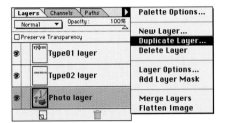

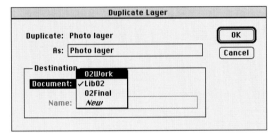

The image is automatically centered in the *02Work.psd* document and the Layers palette for the *02Work.psd* file displays the Photo layer.

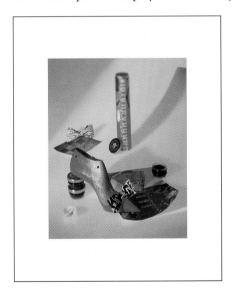

Note: *If the layer size of a source file to be copied is larger than the layer size of the target file, the layer is cropped (not clipped). If the layer size of a source file to be copied is smaller than the layer size of the target file, the contents are centered in the work canvas. A copied layer is not clipped until you save the file.*

3 Save the *02Work.psd* file to *Projects*.

Placing the Type01 image

The Type01 layer in *02Lib.psd* contains an image representing the Russian term for 'shoes' using the Adobe Originals™ font Minion™ Cyrillic.

To create Minion Cyrillic, Adobe designer Robert Slimbach began by researching historical and contemporary Cyrillic typefaces. Like the Latin Minion Cyrillic families, Minion Cyrillic is available is three weights with companion italics, offering the user a large and varied typographic palette. Minion Cyrillic contains a complete set of characters for setting Belarussian, Bulgarian, Macedonian, Russian, Serbo-Croation, and Ukrainian.

Rather than using the Duplicate layer command that you used to copy the Photo layer from *02Lib.psd* to the *02Work.psd* file, you will select and copy the Type01 layer in the *02Lib.psd* file and then paste it to the document window of the *02Work.psd* file.

TIP: WHEN YOU TYPE
THE LAYER NAME OF
A NEW LAYER AND
CLICK OK, THE FLOATING
SELECTION DISAPPEARS
BECAUSE IT IS NO
LONGER NEEDED

1 With the *02Work.psd* file open on the desktop and with the *02Lib.psd* file active, select the Type01 layer in the Layers palette of the *02Lib.psd* file, choose All from the Select menu, and copy it to the Clipboard.

2 With the *02Work.psd* file active, make sure the Photo layer is selected in the Layers palette.

3 Paste the contents of the Clipboard in the *02Work.psd* file.

The Layers palette for the *02Work.psd* file displays a Floating Selection above the Photo layer, and the pasted layer is automatically centered on the work canvas.

Note: Although the Paste Layer command also centers the pasted layer in the document window of the target file, automatically adding a new layer to the target file, our purpose is better served using the Paste command since it adds a floating selection (rather than a new layer).

4 With the *02Work.psd* file active and with the Floating Selection selected in the Layers palette, choose Make Layer from the Layers palette menu, in the Make Layer dialog box type **Type layer** in the Name box, and click OK.

5 Make sure the rulers are displayed.

6 With the Type layer selected in the Layers palette and the move tool selected, drag to position the Type01 image to about ¼ inch below the top of the image and about ½ inch overlapping the right edge of the image as shown in the illustration below.

7 Save the *02Work.psd* file.

Saving selection to a channel

Now that the Type01 image is positioned in the document, you will save the selection to an alpha channel.

1 With the Type layer selected in the Layers palette, choose Load Selection from the Select menu, in the Load Selection dialog box make sure Type layer transparency is selected in the Channel pop-up menu, and click OK.

The Load Selection command loads the opaque areas of a layer as a selection.

2 Choose Save Selection from the Select menu, and in the Save Selection dialog box click OK to accept the defaults.

The Channels palette displays alpha channel #4.

TIP: TO DISPLAY THE RULERS, CHOOSE SHOW RULERS FROM THE WINDOW MENU.

Modifying an alpha channel

After renaming the existing alpha channel in the Channels palette, you will modify it so that it masks the type as well.

1 With the Type layer selected in the Layers palette, select the entire contents of the layer, and press the Delete key.

The Type01 image (black type on white) is deleted from the Type layer.

2 In the Channels palette double-click the alpha channel #4, in the Channel Options dialog box type **Type mask** in the Name box, and click OK.

3 To load the selection saved in the Type mask channel, choose Load Selection from the Select menu, in the Load Selection dialog box make sure Type mask is selected in the Channel pop-up menu, and click OK.

Since the Clipboard still holds a copy of the Type01 layer, you will paste the contents of the Clipboard into the selection you just loaded.

4 In the Channels palette make sure the Type mask channel is selected, and paste the Type01 layer into the selection.

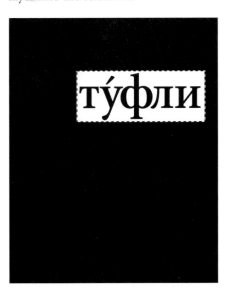

The pasted Type01 image is automatically centered in the selection (in the Type mask channel).

Airbrushing the Type01 selection

After loading the selection in the Type mask channel, you will use the airbrush tool to create the mottled gray effect in the Type01 selection.

1 Select the RGB channel in the Channels palette.

2 Choose Load Selection from the Select menu, in the Load Selection dialog box make sure Type mask channel is selected in the Channel pop-up menu, and click OK.

3 In the Layers palette make sure the Type layer is selected.

4 Double-click the airbrush tool, in the Airbrush Options palette make sure Normal is selected from the Mode pop-up menu, and set the Pressure slider to 20%.

5 In the Brushes palette choose New Brush from the Brushes palette menu, in the New Brush dialog box enter **90** pixels in the Diameter box, **0**% in the Hardness box, and **25**% in the Spacing box, and click OK.

6 With the foreground color set to black, click to spray the paint in smooth strokes to achieve the effect of the mottled gray background in the Type01 image as shown in the illustration below.

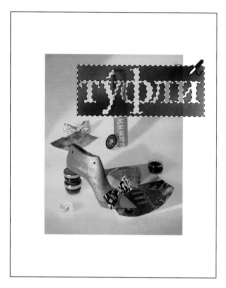

The airbrush effect is applied to selected portions of the layer. If nothing were selected, the airbrush effect could be applied to the entire layer.

Embossing the Type01 selection

The Emboss filter makes a selection appear raised or stamped by suppressing the color within the selection and tracing its edges with black.

1 With the selection saved in the Type mask still loaded, make sure the Type layer is selected in the Layers palette of the *02Work.psd* document.

2 Choose Stylize from the Filter menu and Emboss from the submenu, in the Emboss dialog box position the cursor over the Preview window and drag until the Type01 image is visible, enter **150°** in the Angle box, **5** pixels in the Height box, and **100%** in the Amount box, and click OK.

Like the airbrush effect, the Emboss filter is applied to selected portions of the layer.

3 Save the *02Work.psd* file.

Airbrushing a drop shadow

With the painting mode set to Behind mode, you will use the airbrush tool to draw straight-line drop shadows along the left and bottom edges of the embossed image. When you paint in Behind mode, it appears that you are painting on the *back* of the transparent areas on a sheet of acetate.

Note: *Press the Caps Lock key to toggle between the standard cursor and the precision tool cursor (cross hair) when you want to edit or apply paint with real exactness. The cross hair give you greater accuracy because you can focus the intersection of the cross hairs on the area you want to edit or paint.*

1 Deselect the embossed image, make sure the Type layer is selected in the Layers palette, and make sure the foreground color is set to black.

2 Double-click the airbrush tool, in the Airbrush Options palette choose Behind from the Mode pop-up menu, and make sure the Pressure slider is set to 28%.

3 In the Brushes palette select the 25-pixel, soft-edged brush.

4 To draw the drop shadow on the left edge of the embossed image, click on the left edge of the rectangle about ¼ inch from the top of the rectangle to create a starting point, hold down the Shift key, and click the lower-left corner of the rectangle to create an endpoint.

To draw a drop shadow along the lower edge of the embossed image, you can use the previous endpoint as the starting point for the next drop shadow.

5 Hold down the Shift key, and click about ¼ inch to the left of the lower-right corner of the rectangle.

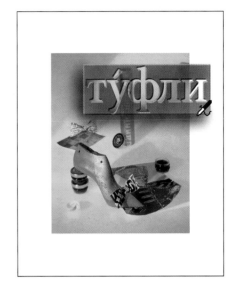

Again, to darken the drop shadow on the lower edge of the embossed image, you can use the previous endpoint as the starting point for the next drop shadow.

6 Hold down the Shift key, and click the lower-left corner of the embossed image.

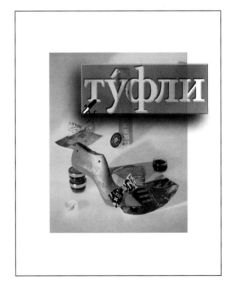

7 Save the *02Work.psd* file.

Drawing a vertical line

You may want to zoom in to a 1:1 view of the *02Final.psd* document in order to view how the vertical line goes "behind" the embossed image.

1 With the Type layer selected in the Layers palette, double-click the line tool, in the Line Tool Options palette choose Behind from the Mode pop-up menu, and enter **1** pixel in the Line Width box.

2 Hold down the Shift key (to constrain the line to a 45° angle), drag from the top of the *02Work.psd* document window, about ½ inch from the right edge of the photo (or about 1 inch from the right edge of the document window) to the bottom of the document window, and release the Shift key to draw the line as shown in the illustration below.

Drawing the 3-D bar

The 3-D bar is actually a rectangle that you will shade to create a dimensional appearance.

1 With the Type layer selected in the Layers palette, double-click the marquee tool, in the Marquee Tool Options palette choose Rectangle from the Shape pop-up menu and Fixed Size from the Style pop-up menu, and enter **360** pixels in the Width box and **10** pixels in the Height box.

2 Click the document window, hold down the mouse button, and drag to position the rectangle about ¼ inch above the bottom of the photo image.

Note: To move an established selection border, hold down the Command key (or the Ctrl key) and the Option key (or the Alt key) and drag the selection border to the desired position.

3 Select the switch color icon in the toolbox to set the foreground color to white.

4 Choose Fill from the Edit menu, in the Fill dialog box make sure the Foreground color is selected from the Use pop-up menu, and click OK to fill the selection with white.

5 Select the default colors icon to set the foreground color to black.

6 Double-click the airbrush tool, in the Airbrush Options palette choose Normal from the Mode pop-up menu, and make sure the pressure is set to 28%.

7 In the Brushes palette choose New Brush from the Brushes palette menu, in the New Brush dialog box enter 7 pixels in the Diameter box, and click OK.

You will shade the 3-D bar so that it appears to have dimension.

8 With the Type layer selected in the Layers palette, click inside the lower-right corner of the rectangle, hold down the Shift key, and click inside the lower-left corner of the rectangle.

9 To darken the straight line shadow, hold down the Shift key and click inside the lower-right corner of the rectangle.

10 To add the final shadowing, click inside the upper-right corner of the rectangle, hold down the Shift key, and click inside the upper-left corner of the rectangle.

Airbrushing a drop shadow

You will use the airbrush tool to draw straight-line drop shadows along the bottom edge of the 3-D bar.

1 Deselect the 3-D bar.

2 With the foreground color set to black, double-click the airbrush tool, in the Airbrush Options palette choose Behind from the Mode pop-up menu, and make sure the pressure is set to 20%.

3 In the Brushes palette select a 20-pixel, soft-edged brush.

4 To draw the drop shadow on the bottom edge of the 3-D bar, below the bottom-right corner of the 3-D bar to create a starting point, hold down the Shift key, and click below the bottom-left corner of the 3-D bar to create an endpoint.

5 Save the *02Work.psd* file.

Placing the Type02 image

Like the Type01 image, the Type02 image was created in Adobe Illustrator, using the Adobe Originals font Minion Cyrillic, and then imported into Adobe Photoshop. The Type02 image represents the Russian term meaning "theater."

So far you have used two methods to copy images from the *02Lib.psd* file to the *02Work.psd* file: the Duplicate Layer command and by copying and pasting a selection to the *02Work.psd* document window. Since it serves our purpose to copy the Type02 image to an existing layer in the *02Work.psd* file, you will select the entire Type02 layer and drag the selection to the *02Work.psd* document, adding a Floating Selection (not a layer) to the Layers palette.

Note: To copy a selection from one file to another file (without adding a new layer to the target file), you can use one of two methods: copying and pasting a selection or dragging a selection from one document to another. Both methods cause the Layers palette of the target file to display a Floating Selection. If you want to add a layer to the target file, use one of three methods: the Duplicate layer command, the Paste layer command, and dragging a layer (from the Layers palette of the source file to the document window of the target file).

1 With the Type layer selected in the Layers palette of the *02Work.psd* file, select the *02Lib.psd* file.

2 With the Type02 layer selected in the Layers palette of the *02Lib.psd* file, select the entire contents of the layer.

3 With the move tool selected, drag the selection from the *02Lib.psd* document window to the *02Work.psd* file document window.

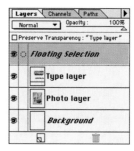

TIP: PRESS THE TAB KEY TO HIDE AND SHOW ALL PALETTES, INCLUD-ING THE TOOLBOX.

The Type02 image is represented in the Layers palette of the *02Work.psd* file as a Floating Selection.

4 With the Info palette open and with the Floating Selection selected in the Layers palette of the *02Work.psd* file, choose Effects from the Image menu and Scale from the submenu.

5 Hold down the Shift key (to scale the selection proportionally) and drag a handle to reduce the Type02 image until the Info palette indicates the percentage change of width and height to be about 85%.

6 Click the gavel icon anywhere inside the selection to confirm the scaling.

7 Drag to position the rectangle so that it is flush with the bottom of the cylinder and its right edge is flush with the one-pixel vertical line.

8 With the Type02 image still selected, make sure the foreground color is set to black, choose Stroke from the Edit menu, in the Stroke dialog box enter 2 pixels in the Width box, click the Inside option in the Location box, and click OK.

9 Deselect the Type02 image.

Airbrushing drop shadows

You will use the airbrush tool to draw straight-line drop shadows behind the left and bottom edges of the central photo image.

1 With the Photo layer selected in the Layers palette of the *Work02* file, make sure the foreground color is set to black.

2 Double-click the airbrush tool, and in the Airbrush Options palette make sure Behind is selected from the Mode pop-up menu and the Pressure slider is set to 28%.

3 In the Brushes palette select the 65-pixel, soft-edged brush.

4 Click ¼ inch below the upper-left corner of the Type02 image to create a starting point, hold down the Shift key, and click the bottom-left corner of the image to create an endpoint.

5 Continue adding the drop shadow effect along the bottom portion of the image as shown in the illustration below.

MERGING LAYERS

To begin a discussion on merging layers, it is best to understand the difference between the Merge Layers command and the Flatten Image command.

The Flatten Image command merges the visible layers into a single Background layer, discarding any hidden layers. The resulting image, consisting of one layer, is known as a flat image. If no background is visible when the Flatten Image command is issued, a white background is merged into the image as well. Most likely you will use the Flatten Image command when you are finished editing a document.

Note: Since each layer requires disk space, merging layers or flattening an image greatly reduces the size of a file, especially important with large documents.

For this example, you will merge the Photo layer and the Type layer, allowing the Background layer to remain intact. Unlike the Flatten Image command, any hidden layers (the Background layer) remain intact.

Note: If all layers are visible, then Merge Layers has the same result as Flatten Image.

1 With everything deselected, in the Layers palette click the eye icon for the Background layer to hide the layer, make sure the eye icons for the Photo layer and Type layer are visible, and make sure one of the layers to be merged is selected in the Layers palette.

Note: One layer to be merged must be selected in the Layers palette, otherwise the Merge Layers command in the Layers palette menu is deactivated.

2 In the Layers palette choose Merge Layers from the Layers palette menu.

By default the newly merged layer is named for the bottom-most layer, Photo layer. The Background layer remains intact.

3 Save the *02Work.psd* file.

Displaying the file size, dimensions, and resolution of a file

Adobe Photoshop displays the file size in the left portion of the lower border (or lower menu bar). You can also display the dimensions, number of channels, and resolution information about a file.

1 To display the file size, choose Document Sizes from the black triangle pop-up menu in the left portion of the bottom border (or bottom menu bar).

The first value indicates the file size of the final flattened file (with all layers merged into one layer, including any channels or paths in the image) as it would be sent to the printer. The second value shows the size of the file as it exists in the document with separate, unmerged layers.

2 To display the dimensions, resolution, and number of channels, position the cursor on the box in the left portion of the lower border (or lower menu bar), hold down the Option key (or the Alt key) and drag to open the file information box.

```
Width: 360 pixels (5 inches)
Height: 443 pixels (6.153 inches)
Channels: 4 (RGB Color)
Resolution: 72 pixels/inch
```

Displaying the scratch disk space

A scratch disk (also called virtual memory) is temporary disk space used for storing data and performing computations on files during a work session when the random-access memory (RAM) is insufficient.

1 Choose Scratch Sizes from the black triangle pop-up menu in the left portion of the bottom border (or bottom menu bar).

The first figure shows how much image data (or space) Adobe Photoshop is using for all open images. The second number shows the amount of RAM available to Adobe Photoshop. When the first number exceeds the second number, there is no more RAM available, and you are using the scratch disk for additional needed memory.

Selecting an interpolation method

When you increase or decrease the file size of an image (by resampling, rotating an image at an arbitrary angle, or using special effects such as skew or perspective), new color values are created for the added pixels. Adobe Photoshop determines the color of added or deleted pixels using the process of *interpolation.*

1 Choose Preferences from the File menu and General from the submenu, in the General Preferences dialog box make sure Bicubic is selected from the Interpolation pop-up menu, and then click OK.

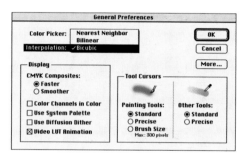

The Bicubic option offers the most precise form of interpolation; however, it is significantly slower than Bilinear interpolation.

Note: The Nearest Neighbor option is the fastest, least precise method; it produces the sharpest results when enlarging a screen grab, as opposed to the Bicubic option, where enlarging a screen grab may produce more jagged results. The Bilinear option produces medium quality that is between the other two options.

Rotating an image

The Rotate command lets you make gradual or dramatic adjustments to all or part of an image.

1 With the Photo layer selected in the Layers palette of the *02Work.psd* file, choose All from the Select menu.

2 Choose Rotate from the Image menu and Arbitrary from the submenu, in the Arbitrary Rotate dialog box enter **15°** in the Angle box, click the CCW option, and click OK.

3 Deselect the image.

4 Click the full screen without menu bar tool in the bottom-right corner of the toolbox to view the results.

5 Click the standard windows tool in the bottom-left corner of the toolbox to return to the normal screen mode.

CREATING VARIATIONS

After defining a repeating pattern for the background image, you will create several variations of this background image using the Difference mode, applying the Ripple filter, and colorizing a layer.

Defining a pattern

Since the image in *02Work.psd* file has been rotated, it will be easier to select a portion of the image from the Photo layer in the *02Lib.psd* file.

1 Choose *02Lib.psd* from the Window menu, and select the Photo layer in the Layers palette, hiding all other layers.

2 Double-click the marquee tool, in the Marquee Options dialog box make sure Rectangle is selected in the Shape pop-up menu and Fixed Size is selected in the Style pop-up menu, and enter **120** pixels in the Width box and **110** pixels in the Height box.

We computed the size of the rectangle by dividing the width (360 pixels) and the height (442 pixels) of the image with the number of tiles we wanted to see across (3) and down (4), respectively.

3 Click, hold down the mouse button, and drag to position the marquee selection around the shoe form, keeping the caviar heel near the left edge of the rectangle as shown in the illustration below.

4 Choose Define Pattern from the Edit menu.

5 Select the Background layer in the Layers palette of the *02Work.psd* file, and select the entire contents of the Background layer.

6 Choose Fill from the Edit menu, in the Fill dialog box choose Pattern from the Use pop-up menu, and click OK.

The Background layer is filled with the shoe pattern.

7 Make sure the Photo layer and the Background layer are displayed (eye icons visible).

8 Close the *02Lib.psd* file.

Setting a layer to Difference mode

Difference mode works on a channel-by-channel basis, setting the resulting color to the absolute value of the difference between the base color and the blend color. The effect of this is that painting with white inverts all colors, while painting with black leaves them untouched. Painting with intermediate colors produces interesting combinations of inversion and darkening.

If you don't mind leaving all this aside for the moment, see if you like the visual effect it produces.

1 With the Background layer selected in the Layers palette, choose Duplicate Layer from the Layers palette menu, in the Duplicate Layer dialog box type **Difference layer** in the Name box, and click OK.

2 Make sure the Difference layer is positioned just above the Background layer in the Layers palette.

3 Click the eye icon to hide the view of the Difference layer.

4 With the Background layer selected in the Layers palette, choose Map from the Image menu and Invert from the submenu to create a negative of the image in the Background layer.

The Background layer thumbnail displays the inverted image.

5 Select the Difference layer in the Layers palette, and choose Difference from the Mode pop-up menu in the Layers palette.

6 Make sure the Difference layer and the Background layer are displayed (eye icons visible) to view the affect of applying Difference mode to the Difference layer.

7 By clicking the eye icon, hide the Difference layer to view a more subtle effect, and then show the Difference layer.

8 Experiment with different modes and multiple Opacity settings to view a variety of effects, and then set the Opacity to 38%.

Note: *Adjusting the mode and opacity only affects the selected layer.*

9 Save the *02Work.psd* file.

Applying the Ripple filter

After duplicating the Difference layer, you will rename the duplicate layer and apply the Ripple filter. The Ripple filter produces an undulating pattern on a selection, like ripples on the surface of a pond.

1 In the Layers palette drag the Difference layer to the New Layer icon in the lower-left corner.

The Layers palette displays the duplicate layer, Difference layer copy.

2 In the Layers palette double-click the duplicate layer (Difference layer copy), in the Layers Option dialog box type **Ripple layer** in the Name box, type **100**% in the Opacity box, choose Normal from the Mode pop-up menu, and click OK.

3 Choose Distort from the Filter menu and Ripple from the submenu, in the Ripple dialog box type **600** in the Amount box; as you view the preview window, experiment with each Size setting (Small, Medium, and Large), select the Medium option, and click OK.

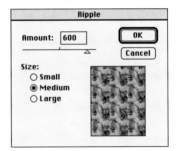

4 In the Layers palette make sure the Ripple layer is positioned just above the Difference layer.

5 With the Ripple layer selected in the Layers palette, try various settings on the Opacity slider in the Layers palette to see a number of effects.

Colorizing a layer

You will use the Hue/Saturation command to adjust the hue and saturation of the background image. Hue is color; saturation is the purity of the color.

1 In the Layers palette drag the Difference layer to the New Layer icon in the lower-left corner.

2 In the Layers palette double-click the duplicate layer (Difference layer copy), in the Layer Options dialog box type **Colorized layer** in the Name box, type **100**% in the Opacity box, choose Normal from the Mode pop-up menu, and click OK.

3 In the Layers palette make sure the Colorized layer is positioned just above the Ripple layer.

4 Choose Adjust from the Image menu and Hue/Saturation from the submenu.

Along the left side of the Hue/Saturation dialog box are six color swatches of the additive and subtractive colors in the order in which they appear on the color wheel. The Sample swatch (at the bottom of the dialog box) shows the current foreground color. You can use the Save buttons to save your color correction settings.

5 In the Hue/Saturation dialog box select the Colorize option to adjust the hue and saturation to fixed values, enter **20** in the Hue box, **28** in the Saturation box, and **0** in the Lightness box, and click OK.

6 With the Colorized layer selected in the Layers palette, make sure it is displayed (eye icon visible), and set the Opacity slider to 80% in the Layers palette to view another effect.

7 Make sure everything is deselected, and save the *02 Work* file.

8 Close all files, and quit (or exit) the Adobe Photoshop application.

3

Using two photographic images, you will compose this photo collage, applying numerous effects throughout. The dancer, almost 6 feet tall, was photographed on a white back-

PHOTOGRAPHIC COLLAGE

ground; the geometric forms, only a few inches tall, were shot on a white background suffused with blue light. ■ Creating this collage provides the opportunity to experiment with a wide array of practical tools and powerful effects. As you execute the steps in this project, you may come to realize the seemingly endless possibilities of Adobe Photoshop. You may see new worlds opening up. You may find more freedom to explore your own vision than you had ever imagined.

This project introduces the Dust & Scratches filter, a new tool that facilitates retouching and photo restoration. This project also introduces the Selective Color command and the Color Range command, powerful new ways to control color.

PHOTOGRAPHIC COLLAGE

The original high resolution image scan is available on the *Advanced Adobe Photoshop* CD-ROM disc. For the sake of reducing the demand for disk space on your system, you will execute this project using a working file with a resolution of 100 ppi.

Project 4 covers:

• Using the Dust & Scratches filter

• Cloning images using the Marquee tool and the Lasso tool

• Using the Selective Color command

• Making a selection in an alpha channel

• Setting the precision tool cursor

• Adjusting the levels of an image

• Applying the Noise filter, the Color Halftone filter, the Wave filter, and the Motion Blur filter

• Using the Posterize command

• Adjusting the Color Balance

• Merging layers

• Making a selection with the Color Range command

• Creating a library of images

• Using the Defringe command and Remove White Matte command

• Linking layers

• Saving a flattened copy of the file.

It should take you about 2 hours to complete this project.

Viewing the final image

1 Before launching the Adobe Photoshop application, throw away the Adobe Photoshop Preferences file to ensure all settings are returned to their default values.

2 Launch the Adobe Photoshop application, and open the *03Final.psd* file in *03Project* to view the final image.

3 Reduce the view of the *03Final.psd* document, and position it in the upper-right corner of your desktop to use as a visual reference.

Opening an Adobe Photoshop file

Rather than creating a new document, you will open the existing Adobe Photoshop file, *Shapes.psd*, and save it as *03Work.psd*.

1 Open the *Shapes.psd* file in *03Project*, and save it to *Projects* as *03Work.psd*.

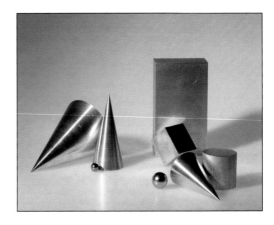

THE DUST & SCRATCHES FILTER

Looking at the standing block and the prone cone, you can see some noticeable scratches. Since it is not uncommon to come across photographs that need retouching, this project will show you a quick method for removing dust and scratches.

The Dust & Scratches filter allows you to specify the parameters by which you can remove the appearance of irregularities in an image.

Removing scratches and dust on the standing block

1 Magnify the view of the standing block.

2 Double-click the lasso tool, and in the Lasso Options palette enter **3** pixels in the Feather box.

3 Drag around an area on the standing block that has scratches and white flecks as shown in the illustration below.

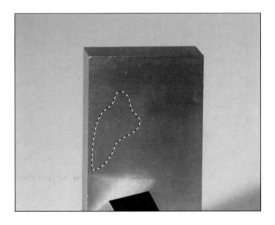

4 Choose Noise from the Filters menu and Dust & Scratches from the submenu, in the Dust & Scratches dialog box position the cursor over the Preview Window, drag until the standing block is visible, click the plus button to magnify the view, enter **2** pixels in the Radius box and **12** levels in the Threshold box, and click OK.

Note: The Radius option determines how far Adobe Photoshop searches to find differing pixels. The image blurs as you increase this option. The Threshold option determines how different the value of pixels need to be in order to be eliminated or altered.

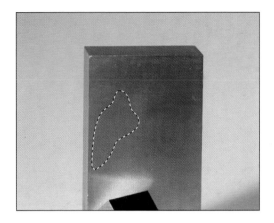

5 Repeat this process on other areas of the standing block.

Note: *Finding the correct compromise between sharpness and concealing the defects require you to try different combinations of radius and threshold settings. If you can't make the image sharp enough, try reducing the selection area around the defect.*

Removing scratches on the prone cone

You can use the Dust & Scratches command to remove the prominent scratches on the prone cone, only this time you will use different settings in the Dust & Scratches dialog box.

TIP: TO TOGGLE BE-
TWEEN THE RECTAN-
GULAR MARQUEE AND
THE ELLIPTICAL MAR-
QUEE, HOLD DOWN THE
OPTION KEY (OR ALT
KEY) AND CLICK THE
MARQUEE TOOL.

1 With the lasso tool selected, drag around one of the prominent scratches on the prone cone.

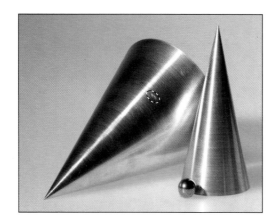

2 With the edges of the selection hidden, choose Noise from the Filters menu, and Dust & Scratches from the submenu.

3 With the Dust & Scratches dialog box displayed, position the cursor in the document window, over the prominent scratch on the prone cone, and click to select that part of the image to be displayed in the Preview window.

4 In the Dust & Scratches dialog box click the plus or minus buttons under the Preview window to magnify or reduce the view of the image, enter **5** pixels in the Radius box and **17** levels in the Threshold box, and click OK.

Note: If part of the image, such as a highlight, seems to become blurred, you can adjust the Radius and Threshold settings, or start again with a smaller, more precise selection of the scratch.

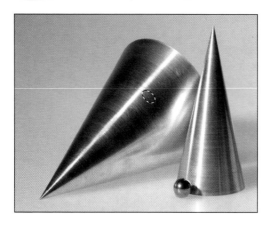

5 Repeat this process for the other prominent scratch on the prone cone.

CLONING IMAGES

You will use the marquee tool and the lasso tool to select images to be copied within the *03Work.psd* document.

Cloning the ball image

1 Double-click the marquee tool, select Elliptical from the Shape pop-up menu, and enter **5** pixels in the Feather box.

2 Position the cursor in the center of the large silver ball, hold down the Option key (or Alt key) and the Shift key, and drag until the cursor is about one-sixteenth inch outside of the ball, selecting some of the blue background.

3 Hold down the Option key (or Alt key) and drag a duplicate silver ball to the left about one-half inch from the original ball as shown in the illustration below.

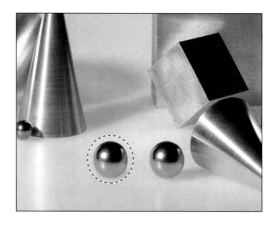

Airbrushing a drop shadow

After selecting a color from an existing shadow in the image, you will paint a shadow for the duplicated silver ball.

1 Choose Inverse from the Select menu to select everything other than the duplicated ball.

2 With the edges of the selection hidden, double-click the airbrush tool, and in the Airbrush Options palette set the Pressure slider to the **30%** setting.

3 In the Brushes palette select the 13-pixel, soft-edged brush, third from the left in the second row.

4 Make sure the Caps Lock key is not held down.

5 Hold down the Option key (or Alt key) to display the cursor as an eyedropper tool, and click the shadow to the right of the original ball.

The foreground color is set to the color of the pixel selected in the shadow.

6 Release the Option key (or Alt key) and paint a shadow for the duplicated ball as shown in the illustration below.

7 Deselect the ball, and save the *03Work.psd* file.

CLONING THE STANDING CONE

After selecting the standing cone with the lasso tool, you will use the Paste Into command to paste the standing cone behind the large prone cone.

Note: *The bottom edge of the standing cone will be obscured by the large prone cone, so it is not necessary to make a precise selection of the standing cone.*

1 Double-click the lasso tool, and in the Lasso Options palette enter **0** pixels in the Feather box.

2 Hold down the Option key (or Alt key), click the three corners of the standing cone, and then click the first corner to close the selection to draw three straight-line segments as shown in the illustration below.

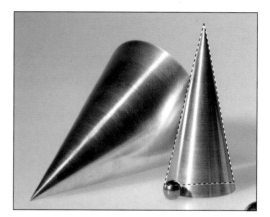

3 Copy the selected cone.

Next, you will select the large prone cone and inverse the selection so that you can paste the copy of the standing cone behind it using the Paste Into command.

4 Again, to draw the three straight-line segments as shown in the illustration below, make sure the lasso tool is selected, hold down the Option key (or Alt key), click the three corners of the large prone cone and click the first corner to close the selection.

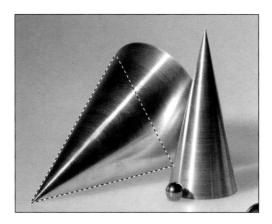

5 Inverse the selection, making it possible to paste the copied cone into the selection.

6 Choose Paste Into from the Edit menu, and drag to position the standing cone so that it is positioned "behind" the prone cone, with its lower edge obscured as shown in the illustration below.

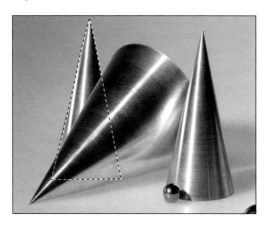

7 Deselect the cone.

THE SELECTIVE COLOR COMMAND

Adobe Photoshop allows you to color correct by modifying the amount of ink used to make a specific color. In this example, you will use the Selective Color command to increase the amount of magenta, yellow, and black to create a deeper, more vibrant color.

Note: You must be in the composite RGB channel to use the Selective Color command.

1 Choose All from the Select menu.

2 Choose Adjust from the Image menu and Selective Color from the submenu, in the Selective Color dialog box click the Preview option, choose Cyan from the Colors pop-up menu, make sure the Method option is set to Relative, and enter the following settings:

Cyan 0
Magenta 90
Yellow 18
Black 25

3 Click OK to close the dialog box.

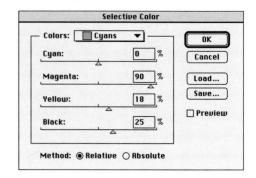

Note: Relative adjusts the existing CMYK values. For example, if you add 10% magenta to a pixel that is 50% magenta, the magenta ink is set to 55%. Absolute adjusts the colors in absolute values. For example, if you increase the magenta by 10% for a pixel that is 50% magenta, the magenta ink is set to 60%.

4 Deselect everything, and save the *03Work.psd* file.

MAKING A SELECTION IN AN ALPHA CHANNEL

Adobe Photoshop provides several tools for selecting parts of an image: the marquee tool, the lasso tool, the magic wand tool, the Color Range command, and the pen tool in the Paths palette.

While these selection tools allow you to make selections in a variety of ways, this exercise expands on how to use an alpha channel for making a selection as well. It may help to remember that every selection is a mask since its limits change to the selected area. You use a mask to isolate an area that you want to protect from change.

The goal of this exercise is to mask the shapes in such a way that they seem more like a skyline. With the mask protecting the shapes, it will be possible to apply the Cloud filter to the background without affecting the skyline of shapes.

Creating an alpha channel

Although it is possible to use the pen tool to select the shapes, you may find it easier to make a selection using a duplicate channel. For this reason, it's best to duplicate the channel that has the most contrast between the edges of the shapes and the background, allowing you to build the mask with the greatest ease.

1 In the Channels palette, click the Red, Green, and Blue channels to view them independently.

The Blue channel has the most contrast between the edges of the shapes and the background.

2 With the Blue channel selected, choose Duplicate Channel from the Channels palette menu, in the Duplicate Channel dialog box type **Horizon mask** in the Name box, and click OK.

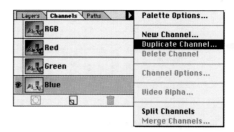

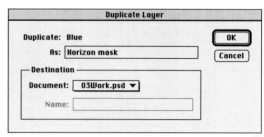

Note: To duplicate an existing channel, drag the channel in the Channels palette to the New Channel icon, the middle icon in the bottom of the Channels palette.

Modifying an alpha channel

After using the Threshold command to make a rough selection of the shapes, you will refine the selection using the lasso tool, the marquee tool and the paintbrush tool.

The Threshold command allows you to specify a certain level as a threshold. All pixels lighter than the threshold are converted to white. All pixels darker than the threshold are converted to black.

1 With the Horizon mask channel selected in the Channels palette, choose Map from the Image menu and Threshold from the submenu, and in the Threshold dialog box drag the Threshold Level slider to about 200, watching the effect as you drag.

2 Adjust the Threshold Level slider to its optimum position where the edges of the selection are mostly distinct from the immediate background as shown in the illustration below, and click OK.

3 With the lasso tool selected, drag a rough selection over the horizon that includes the top two-thirds of the document.

Note: Drag the lasso tool outside of the document window to ensure all pixels near the border of the document window are selected.

4 Press the Delete key to delete the contents of the selection.

5 Deselect the background area, and make sure the Horizon mask channel is still selected in the Channels palette.

6 Double-click the marquee tool, in the Marquee Options palette choose Rectangular from the Shape pop-up menu, and make sure the Feather is set to 0 pixels.

7 Drag to select the lower-third portion of the document as shown in the illustration below.

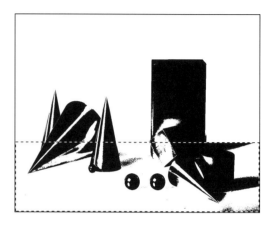

8 With the foreground color set to black, fill the selection with black to mask it.

9 Deselect the rectangle, select the Horizon mask channel in the Channels palette.

10 In the Channels palette make sure the RGB channel is displayed (eye icon visible).

The document window displays the RGB image with a red overlay indicating the masked portions of the selection.

Setting the precision tool cursor

To refine the selection with greater precision, you will change the cursor to a cross hair and paint the unmasked portions of the shapes.

1 Choose Preferences from the File menu and General from the submenu, in the General Preferences dialog box click the Precise option under Painting Tools, and click OK.

Note: If you do not override the standard cursor display, press the Caps Lock key to switch between the standard cursor and the precision cursor.

2 Click the paintbrush tool, and in the Brushes palette choose a 5-pixel, hard-edged brush (third from the left in the top row).

3 Paint the unmasked areas of the shapes that extend above the horizon, completely masking them as shown in the illustration below.

Note: Paint with white to "erase" the mask.

4 Save the *03Work.psd* file.

Applying the Difference Clouds filter to an alpha channel

After loading the selection from the Horizon mask channel, you will apply the Difference Clouds filter to the selected area in the Horizon mask channel.

1 With the Horizon mask channel selected in the Channels palette, choose Load Selection from the Select menu, in the Load Selection dialog box make sure Horizon mask channel is selected in the Channel pop-up menu, and click OK.

The sky portion of the image (above the horizon) is selected.

2 Choose Render from the Filter menu and Difference Clouds from the submenu.

The Difference Clouds filter is applied to the selection, modifying the Horizon mask channel.

Adjusting the levels of the selection

After loading the selection in the Horizon mask channel, you will use the Levels dialog box to adjust the levels of the selected portions of the image, darkening the lighter areas, which causes the cloud formations to look more realistic and patchy.

The Levels dialog box allows you to adjust to the brightness, contrast, and gamma (midtones) in an image.

1 With the RGB channel selected in the Channels palette, choose Load Selection from the Select menu to load the mask, in the Load Selection dialog box make sure the *03Work.psd* file is selected in the Document pop-up menu and the Horizon mask channel is selected in the Channel pop-up menu, and click OK.

2 With the edges of the selection hidden, choose Adjust from the Image menu and Levels from the submenu.

The histogram in the Levels dialog box indicates that the image has an abundance of high tones (whites) and low tones (blacks) with some midtones as well that represent the light gray tones running throughout the image.

TIP: TO LOAD A
CHANNEL AS A
SELECTION, HOLD
DOWN THE OPTION
KEY (OR ALT KEY)
AND CLICK THE CHAN-
NEL CONTAINING
THE SELECTION TO BE
LOADED. OR, DRAG
THE CHANNEL TO
THE LOAD SELEC-
TION ICON IN THE
LOWER-LEFT CORNER
OF THE CHANNELS
PALETTE.

You can use the slider controls directly below the histogram to increase the contrast in an image, or you can enter the values directly into the Input levels boxes.

3 In the Levels dialog box make sure the RGB channel is selected in the Channel pop-up menu, type **0, 1.00,** and **189** in the Input Levels boxes to darken the image.

You can use the slider controls at the bottom of the Levels dialog box to decrease the contrast in an image, or you can enter the values directly into the Output levels boxes.

4 Drag the left-most black triangle on the Output Levels slider to setting 83 to reduce the contrast in the image, and click OK.

The adjusted levels are applied to the selected areas in the image as shown in the illustration below.

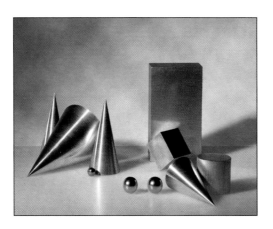

5 Deselect the background, and save the *03Work.psd* file.

CREATING THE VISUAL TRANSITIONS IN THE IMAGE

To create the transitions you see in the image, you will apply four filters to selected areas on a new layer, and then merge the layer with the Background layer.

As you apply these filters, be sure to preview how various settings affect your image before you apply the filter. Since Adobe Photoshop 3.0 makes it possible to see in advance what an image will look like, you'll save time and get perfect results.

Adding a new layer

After selecting and floating a portion of the Background layer, you will create a new layer from the floating selection.

1 Double-click the marquee tool, in the Marquee Options palette, make sure Rectangular is selected from the Shape pop-up menu, and enter **30** pixels in the Feather box.

2 With the Background layer selected in the Layers palette of the *03Work.psd* file, select about one-fourth of the document on the right side as shown in the illustration below.

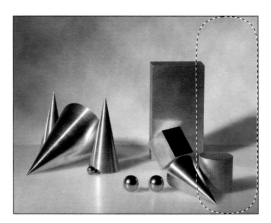

Feathering causes the edges of the selection to be rounded.

3 Choose Float from the Select menu.

4 In the Layers palette drag the Floating Selection to the New Layer icon in the lower-left corner, in the Make Layer dialog box type **Composite layer** in the Name box, and click OK.

Note: A Floating Selection is defloated when another layer in the Layers palette is selected.

Desaturating the color in the image

After selecting the image on the Composite layer, you will use the Hue/Saturation dialog box to completely desaturate the color in the image.

1 With the Composite layer selected in the Layers palette, choose All from the Select menu, and then Float from the Select menu.

2 Choose Adjust from the Image menu and Hue/Saturation from the submenu, in the Hue/Saturation dialog box set Saturation to -100 to make the selection gray, and click OK.

Note: A desaturated RGB image looks like a gray-scale image.

Applying the Noise filter

The Noise filter subtly blurs a selection by adding pixels to make the selection blend into the surrounding pixels. Noise in an image is represented by pixels with randomly distributed color levels.

1 With the Composite layer selected in the Layers palette, choose Noise from the Filter menu and Add Noise from the submenu, and click OK to accept the default settings.

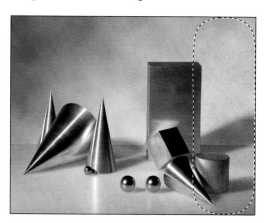

Using the Posterize command

The Posterize command lets you specify the number of gray levels (or brightness values) for an image and then maps pixels to the level that is the closest match. The effects of this command are most evident when you reduce the number of gray levels in a grayscale image; however, you can also use this command to produce some interesting effects in color images.

1 With the Background layer selected in the Layers palette, drag to select about one-fourth of the document, slightly overlapping the previous selection as shown in the illustration below.

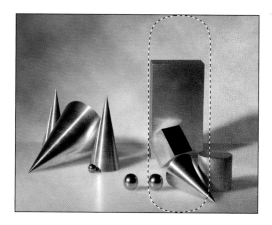

2 Choose Float from the Select menu, and in the Layers palette drag the Floating Selection to be above the Composite Layer.

3 With the Floating Selection selected in the Layers palette, choose Map from the Image menu and Posterize from the submenu, in the Posterize dialog box enter **10** in the Levels box, and click OK.

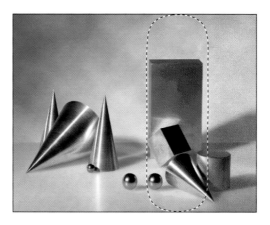

Applying the Color Halftone filter

The Color Halftone filter simulates the effect on a selection by displacing pixels, and by finding and heightening contrast in an image.

1 With the Background layer selected in the Layers palette, drag to select about one-fourth of the document, slightly overlapping the previous selection as shown in the illustration below.

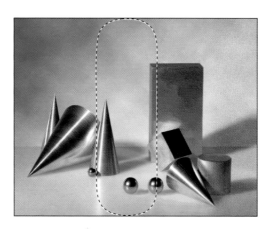

2 Choose Float from the Select menu, and in the Layers palette drag the Floating Selection to be above the Composite Layer.

The Layers palette displays the Floating Selection as selected.

3 Choose Pixelate from the Filter menu and Color Halftone from the submenu, in the Color Halftone enter **4** pixels in the Maximum radius box (for the size of a halftone dot), and click OK.

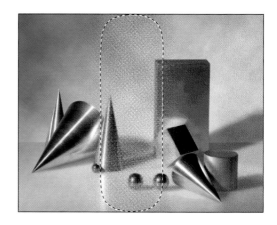

Applying the Wave filter

The Wave filter distorts an image somewhat randomly, but gives you greater control over the results.

1 With the Background layer selected in the Layers palette, drag to select about one-fourth of the document, slightly overlapping the previous selection as shown in the illustration below.

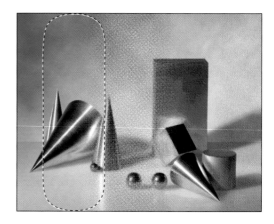

2 With the Background layer selected in the Layers palette, choose Float from the Select menu, and in the Layers palette drag the Floating Selection to be above the Composite Layer.

The Layers palette displays the Floating Selection as selected.

3 Choose Distort from the Filter menu and Wave from the submenu, in the Wave dialog box enter **3** in the Number of Generators box, enter **5** and **100** for the minimum and maximum wavelength (to set the distance from one wave crest to the next), enter **1** and **15** for the minimum and maximum amplitude (to set the height of the wave), click the Randomize button two times, and click OK.

box make sure the Midtones option is selected, in the Color Levels boxes enter **23** to add Red, **61** to add Magenta, and **59** to add Blue, and click OK.

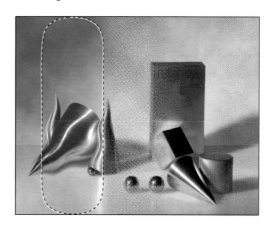

2 Deselect the image.

MERGING LAYERS

While you are creating a composite image, it is useful to keep individual elements on separate layers. When you are finished editing two or more layers, it is possible to merge them into a single layer, reducing the file size of your document.

Note: *Since each layer requires disk space, merging layers is especially important when you are working in large documents.*

1 Make sure the eye icon is visible for both layers.

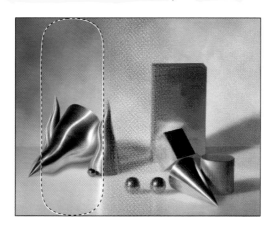

4 Save the *03Work.psd* file.

ADJUSTING THE COLOR BALANCE

Use the Color Balance command to change the mixture of colors in a color image. Use this command to delete unwanted colors from an image or to enhance a dull or muted color.

1 With the Wave selection still selected, choose Adjust from the Image menu and Color Balance from the submenu, in the Color Balance dialog

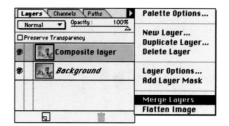

TIP: TO SELECT THE
PLUS EYEDROPPER
TOOL, HOLD DOWN
THE SHIFT KEY AS
YOU CLICK IN THE
DOCUMENT WIN-
DOW OR IN THE
PREVIEW WINDOW.

2 In the Layers palette choose Merge Layers from the Layers palette menu.

The visible layers are shown to be merged into the Background layer.

3 Save the *03Work.psd* file.

USING THE COLOR RANGE COMMAND

After making a selection of the white background of an image using the Color Range command, you will inverse the selection in order to select the dancer image.

Unlike the magic wand tool which selects adjacent pixels, the Color Range command selects a specified color anywhere that it appears in the image. You can choose from a preset range of colors, or you can build the selection by sampling colors from the image.

Note: In addition to basing selections on sampled colors and a fuzziness value, the Color Range command allows you to build a selection or a mask based on numerous options, such as a collection of colors, selected tonal quality (highlights, midtones, or shadows), or selected colors in an RGB or Lab image lying outside the CMYK gamut.

1 Open the *Dancer.psd* file in *03Project*.

2 Choose Color Range from the Select menu, in the Color Range dialog box make sure the Selection option is selected (to see the selected areas in the Preview window), make sure Sampled Colors is selected from the Select pop-up menu, make sure Fuzziness is set to 40, choose None from the Selection Preview pop-up menu, and click the upper portion of the white background of the image in the document window or in the Preview window.

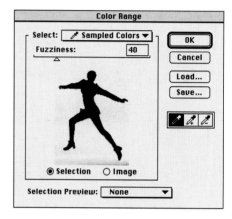

Note: Selecting the Selection option (as opposed to the Image option) allows you to view the selection as you build it.

Looking at the Preview window in the Color Range dialog box, you can see the figure of the dancer is completely unselected, black indicating the unselected areas. Looking further, you can also see some dark areas at the bottom of the image, indicating parts of the background not selected.

3 Drag the Fuzziness slider to the right and notice how as the dark areas at the bottom of the image vanish, the lightest portions of the dancer become selected (or white).

Rather than adjusting the fuzziness, it works best in this example to select additional colors with the plus eyedropper tool.

TIP: TO DUPLICATE A LAYER, DRAG IT TO THE NEW LAYER ICON IN THE LOWER-LEFT CORNER OF THE LAYERS PALETTE.

4 Set the Fuzziness slider to 40, select the plus eye-dropper tool in the Color Range dialog box, click the dark areas at the bottom of the document until they are white (completely selected) in the Preview window, and click OK.

The document window displays the image with the selected white background.

CREATING A LIBRARY OF IMAGES

You may recall how in the previous project you opened the library of images and copied images found on separate layers to your working document. Although a library of images provides the means to organize separate images in a single file, it is not meant to serve as a working file for composing or processing an image.

Placing the dancer image in its own library of images

In this example, establishing your own library of images involves saving the *Dancer.psd* file as *Library.psd*, placing the dancer image on a transparent layer, and hiding the default Background layer.

1 With the *Dancer.psd* file active, save the file as *Library.psd* to *Projects*.

2 With the white background still selected in the document window, press the Delete key to delete the contents of the selection.

The background still appears to be white because the Background layer has an opaque (white) background. For this reason, you will place the dancer image on a layer with a transparent background.

3 Choose Inverse from the Select menu to select the dancer image.

4 Choose Float from the Select menu to float the selection.

To view the image in your library with a transparent background, you will make a layer from the floating selection, and then hide the original Background layer.

5 In the Layers palette choose Make Layer from the Layers palette menu, in the Make Layer dialog box type **Dancer layer** in the Name box, and click OK.

The Layers palette displays the Dancer layer.

6 Hide the Background layer, and save the *Library.psd* file.

CLEANING UP AN IMAGE

You will use the Defringe command and the Remove White Matte command to clean up the edges of the dancer image.

Before cleaning up the edges, you will create a black background to better illustrate the process.

1 With the *Library.psd* file active, select the Background layer (which automatically shows it) in the Layers palette, and fill the entire layer with black.

2 Select the Dancer layer in the Layers palette, make sure the Background layer is displayed (eye icon visible), and hide the edges of the selection of the dancer image.

It is possible to view a white halo around the image, caused from the object being photographed against a white background.

Defringing a selection

The Defringe command replaces the color of any "fringe" pixels with the colors of nearby pixels that contain pure colors (pure color pixels do not contain any of the background color). For example, if you select a white object on a blue background and move the selection, some of the blue background is moved with the object. The Defringe command removes the blue pixels.

1 Make sure the Dancer layer is selected in the Layers palette.

2 Choose Matting from the Select menu and Defringe from the submenu, in the Defringe dialog box enter **1** pixel (the distance used to find replacement pixels) in the Width box, and click OK.

Removing white matte from a selection

Pasting an image that was originally created on a white background often results in background pixels remaining along the edges of a selection. The Remove White Matte command allows you to eliminate the remnants (ghosting) of white around the edges.

1 Make sure the Dancer layer is selected in the Layers palette.

2 Choose Matting from the Select menu and Remove White Matte from the submenu.

3 Drag the Background layer to the Trash icon in the lower-right corner of the Layers palette to delete it.

4 Deselect the dancer image, and save the *Library.psd* file.

PLACING THE DANCERS

You will place the four dancers on four separate layers, adjusting the opacity for each layer.

Placing the first dancer

You will drag the Dancer layer in the *Library.psd* file to the *03Work.psd* file, and then duplicate the image three more times to place four dancer images on four separate layers in the *03Work.psd* file.

1 With the *03Work.psd* file open and with the *Library.psd* file active, drag the Dancer layer from the Layers palette of the *Library.psd* file to the document window of the *03Work.psd* file.

The Layers palette for the *03Work.psd* file displays the Dancer layer.

2 With the move tool selected and with the Dancer layer selected in the Layers palette for the *03Work.psd* file, drag to position the right-most dancer about ½ inch from the right edge of the *03Work.psd* document and about 1 inch above the bottom edge as shown in the illustration below.

3 Double-click the Dancer layer in the Layers palette, in the Layer Options dialog box type **30%** in the Opacity box, and click OK.

4 Close the *Library.psd* file, and save the *03Work.psd* file.

Placing the second dancer

1 With the *03Work.psd* file active, drag the Dancer layer to the New Layer icon in the lower-left corner of the Layers palette to duplicate the layer.

The Layers palette displays the Dancer layer copy at the top of the stack of layers.

2 With the Dancer layer selected in the Layers palette, type **5** to specify an opacity setting of 50%.

3 With the move tool selected and with the Dancer layer copy selected in the Layers palette, drag in the document window to position the second dancer about ⅛ inch above and about 1 inch to the left of the first dancer.

Placing the third dancer

1 With the *03Work.psd* file active, drag the Dancer layer copy to the New Layer icon in the lower-left corner of the Layers palette.

The Layers palette displays the new layer, Dancer layer copy 2, at the top of the stack of layers.

2 With the Dancer layer copy 2 selected in the Layers palette, type **7** to specify an opacity setting of 70%.

3 With the move tool selected and with the Dancer layer copy 2 selected in the Layers palette, drag in the document window to position the third dancer about ¼ inch below and about 1 inch to the left of the second dancer.

Placing the fourth dancer

1 With the *03Work.psd* file active, drag the Dancer layer (or any Dancer layer) to the New Layer icon in the lower-left corner of the Layers palette.

2 Make sure the Dancer layer copy 3 has an opacity setting of 100%.

3 With the move tool selected and with the Dancer layer copy 3 selected in the Layers palette, drag in the document window to position the fourth dancer about 1½ inch below and about 1½ inch to the left of the third dancer.

Linking layers

While it is possible to move layers independently, you can also link multiple layers and move them together.

1 With the Dancer layer copy 3 selected in the Layers palette, click the second column from the left in the Dancer layer copy 2 to link the two layers.

The link icons appear in the second column from the left.

2 Click the second column from the left for the two remaining Dancer layers.

3 With the move tool selected, drag the linked layers as one unit in the document window in any direction.

4 In the Layers palette click the second column in the Dancer layer copy 3 to unlink all layers.

Applying the Motion Blur filter

The Motion Blur filter produces a blur effect in a particular direction and of a specific intensity. The effect of this filter is analogous to taking a picture of a moving object with an extended exposure time.

1 Double-click the lasso tool, and in the Lasso Options palette enter **3** pixels in the Feather box.

2 Make sure Dancer layer copy 3 is selected in the Layers palette.

3 With the lasso tool selected, hold down the Shift key (to make multiple selections), and select the upper arms and the back of the legs.

4 Choose Blur from the Filter menu and Motion Blur from the submenu, in the Motion Blur dialog box select the Preview option, position the cursor over the Preview window, drag to view a portion of the figure to be blurred, enter **60°** in the Angle box and **8** pixels in the Distance box, and click OK.

5 Deselect the selection, and save the *03Work.psd* file.

USING THE SAVE A COPY COMMAND

The Save a Copy command lets you save a copy of a file without replacing or affecting the current open file you are working in. When you use the Save a Copy command you specify how to save the file: with all its channels and layers intact; or as a flattened version of the file, where all visible layers have been merged. You can also choose to delete any alpha channels in the file, resulting in a much smaller file that you can use to export the final image.

Note: Adobe Photoshop files must be flattened before being sent to the imagesetter. You can print an unflattened file in Adobe Photoshop; only visible layers will be printed.

Saving a flattened copy

After using the Save a Copy command to save a flattened version of the *03Work.psd* file to *Projects*, you will continue editing the current open file, *03Work.psd*.

1 In the Layers palette make sure all layers are displayed (eye icons visible), and choose Save a Copy from the File menu.

Note: Any layers that are not displayed will not be included in the saved, flattened version.

2 When prompted, make sure *Projects* is selected in the pop-up menu, type **03Flat** in the Name box, click the Flatten Image option, and click Save (or OK).

The five layers are now merged into the Background layer for the *03Flat* file.

Softening the edges of the document

With your current file still intact, it's possible to add a finishing touch to this document. You will soften the edges by deleting a border selected with a 30-pixel feather.

1 Double-click the marquee tool, in the Marquee Options palette make sure Rectangle is selected in the Shape pop-up menu, and enter **15** pixels in the Feather box.

2 With the Background layer selected in the Layers palette, drag to create a marquee selection within one-fourth inch of the outer edge of the working canvas as shown in the illustration below.

3 Choose Inverse from the Select menu to select the border.

4 Press the Delete key to delete the border.

5 Deselect the border, and save the *03Work.psd* file.

6 Close open files, and quit (or exit) the Adobe Photoshop application.

4

In this project you will create the magazine advertisement that promotes a new fragrance called "kyphi," named for the incense that the Egyp-

PERFUME ADVERTISEMENT

tians offered to Ra, the sun god, at the end of each day. ■ To draw even more inspiration from that place and time, we based the overall design of the bottle on the perfume flasks of ancient Egypt. Using **Adobe Dimensions**, a 3-D design application, it was possible to create the bottle, stopper, and floating ribbon images, and then import each image into Adobe Photoshop in **EPS file** format with a scan resolution of 200 ppi. While this resolution would be desirable for a magazine ad, you will execute the necessary steps using a working resolution of 130 ppi.

Adobe Garamond, the typeface featured in this project, is an Adobe Originals typeface. Some of the most popular typefaces in history are those based on the types of the sixteenth-century printer, publisher, and type designer Claude

PERFUME ADVERTISEMENT

Garamond, whose sixteenth-century types were modeled on those of the Venetian printers from the end of the previous century. Adobe designer Robert Slimbach went to the Plantin-Moretus museum in Antwerp, Belgium, to study the original Garamond typefaces. This served as the basis for the design of the Adobe Garamond romans; the italics are based on types by Robert Granjon, a contemporary of Garamond's. This elegant, versatile design, the first Adobe Originals typeface, was released in 1989, and includes three weights, plus a titling font, alternate characters, and an Expert Collection to provide a flexible family of text types.

This project covers:

• Customizing the Commands palette

• Adding and editing a layer mask

• Viewing the mask channel in the document window

• Saving and loading color correction settings from the Hue/Saturation dialog box

• Applying the Emboss filter

• Using the Scale command, the Flip command, and the Rotate command

• Moving linked layers in the document window as one unit.

It should take you about 2 hours to complete this project.

Viewing the final image

1 Before launching the Adobe Photoshop application, throw away the Adobe Photoshop Preferences file to ensure all settings are returned to their default values.

2 Make sure the Adobe Garamond font, found on the *Advanced Adobe Photoshop* CD-ROM disc, is installed.

3 Launch the Adobe Photoshop application, and open the *04Final.psd* file in *04Project* to view the final image.

The Layers palette contains entries for the Background layer and the six layers used to create this document. The mode and opacity for the selected layer, Bottle layer, are also displayed.

4 Reduce the view of the *04Final.psd* document, and position it in the upper-right corner of your desktop to use as a visual reference.

THE COMMANDS PALETTE

When you are working on a keyboard that has function keys, you can use the Commands palette to choose frequently used commands.

In addition to adding new commands to the Commands palette, you can change the assignment of a command and reorder the commands in the Commands palette.

Editing a command in the Commands palette

You will change a preassigned command by assigning the Hide/Show Edges command to the F1 function key.

The Hide/Show Edges command toggles back and forth, allowing you to temporarily hide or show the edges of a selection border.

1 With the Commands palette open, choose Edit Commands from the Commands palette menu, in the Edit Commands dialog box make sure the F1 function key is selected, and click the Change button.

2 In the Change Command dialog box choose Hide/Show Edges from the Select menu, make sure F1 is selected from the Function Key pop-up menu, choose Red from the Color pop-up menu, and click OK.

Note: A single color can be used to identify related commands.

3 In the Edit Commands dialog box click OK to apply the change.

Note: In the Edit Commands dialog box drag a command up or down in the list to rearrange the order of the commands.

The Commands palette displays the newly assigned function key.

CREATING A DOCUMENT

The *04Lib.psd* file contains the images you will copy to the your working file, *04Work.psd*, to compose the perfume advertisement.

Opening a new document

1 Create a new document, and in the New dialog box, type **04Work.psd** in the Name box, enter **5** inches in the Width box, **7** inches in the Height box, and **130** pixels per inch in the Resolution box, make sure RGB color is selected from the Mode pop-up menu, and click OK.

Placing the sky image

After dragging a selected image from the *04Lib.psd* file to the *04Work.psd* file, you will rotate and position the sky image.

TIP: DOUBLE-CLICK
THE HAND TOOL TO
MAKE THE IMAGE FIT
IN THE WINDOW.

1 Open the *04Lib.psd* file found in *04Project*.

Consisting of five separate images on transparent layers, this library of images organizes the components of the project, allowing you to copy the images to your working document.

2 Select the Photo layer in the Layers palette, displaying the photo image in the document window, and make sure all other layers in the library are hidden.

3 With the rectangular marquee tool selected, drag to marquee select the entire sky, without including any portion of the ruins as shown in the illustration below.

4 With the cursor positioned on the selection in the document window of the *04Lib.psd* file, drag it to the document window of the *04Work.psd* file.

The Layers palette of the *04Work.psd* file displays a Floating Selection.

5 To rotate the selection to the upright position, choose Rotate from the Image menu and 90° CW from the submenu.

6 Choose Hide Edges from the Select menu to hide the edges of the selection.

7 Drag the sky image until its edges are aligned with the edges of the upper-right corner of the document window.

Duplicating the sky image

After duplicating, flipping, and positioning the sky image, you will select the double sky image and scale it to fill the entire work canvas.

1 With the sky image still selected, hold down the Option key (or Alt key) and the Shift key (to constrain the movement to 45° or 90°) as you drag away from the sky image to the left to create a duplicate sky image.

2 With the duplicate sky image selected, choose Flip from the Image menu and Horizontal from the submenu.

3 Before aligning the right edge of the duplicate sky image to be flush with the left edge of the first image, zoom in twice to magnify the view of the document.

4 With the edges of the selection hidden, drag the duplicate image so that its right edge is flush with the left edge of the original image as shown in the illustration below.

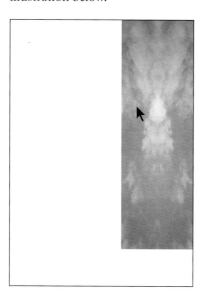

Scaling a selection

After selecting the entire sky image, you will scale the image so that it fills the work canvas.

1 Click the Zoom to Screen button in the Zoom Tool Options palette to set the document window to the largest size that can fit on your monitor and still contain the entire work canvas.

2 With the magic wand tool selected, click the white background in the document window to select it, deselecting the duplicated sky image.

3 Choose Inverse from the Select menu to select the entire sky image.

4 Choose Effects from the Image menu and Scale from the submenu.

5 Drag the bottom-left handle of the image to the bottom-left corner of the window.

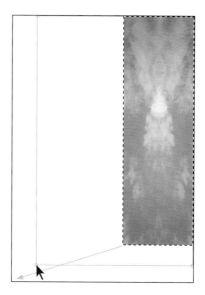

6 With the cursor displayed as a gavel icon, click anywhere inside the selection to confirm the scaling.

Note: *Click anywhere outside of a selection to cancel the scaling.*

7 Save the *04Work.psd* file.

Placing the bottle image

You will use the Duplicate Layer command to copy the Bottle layer from the *04Lib.psd* file to the *04Work.psd* file. The Duplicate Layer command adds a new layer to the *04Work.psd* file, and centers the duplicate layer in the target document.

Note: *Rather than automatically centering a duplicate layer in a target file, dragging a layer (from the Layers palette of a source file) to the document window (of a target file) positions the duplicate layer where you release the mouse button.*

Time out for a movie

 If your system is capable of running Adobe Teach movies, you can see a preview of the technique used to create the bottle image in Adobe Dimensions. Play the movie named 3-D Bottle. For information on how to play Adobe Teach movies, see the "What You Need To Do" section at the beginning of this book.

1 With the *04Lib.psd* file active, deselect all selections, and select the Bottle layer in the Layers palette.

Note: *If you want to select a layer without clicking the layer in the Layers palette, make sure the desired layer is displayed (eye icon visible), select the move tool, hold down the Command key (or Ctrl key), position the cursor in the document window over the image on the desired layer, and click. The lower the opacity setting of the desired layer, the more likely you will select the layer behind it.*

2 Choose Duplicate Layer from the Layers palette menu, in the Duplicate Layer dialog box choose the *04Work.psd* file from the Document pop-up menu in the Destination box, and click OK.

The Layers palette for the *04Work.psd* file displays the Bottle layer, and the document window displays the centered bottle image.

3 With the move tool selected, hold down the Shift key (constraining the movement to a 45° angle), and drag the bottle image down in the document window to position it about 1 inch below the top edge of the work canvas.

Setting the Bottle layer to Multiply mode

Setting the Bottle layer to Multiply mode means that the Adobe Photoshop application will multiply the color information in the Background layer by the color information in the Bottle layer, which will produce a darker color.

For example, multiplying a color with black always produces black, and multiplying a color with white leaves the color unchanged. If you were painting in Multiply mode with a color other than black or white, successive strokes with a painting tool would produce progressively darker colors, much like drawing on an image with multiple magic markers.

1 In the Layers palette make sure the Bottle layer for the *04Work.psd* file is selected, and choose Multiply from the Mode pop-up menu.

The Background layer seems to appear through the Bottle layer.

Note: If the results of setting a layer to Multiply mode seem too dark, try lowering the opacity setting for the layer.

Placing the stopper image

Again, you will use the Duplicate Layer command to copy the Stopper layer from the *04Lib.psd* file to the *04Work.psd* file, adding a new layer to the *04Work.psd* file, and centering the duplicate layer in the target document.

1 With the *04Lib.psd* file active, select the Stopper layer in the Layers palette, hiding all other layers.

2 In the Layers palette choose Duplicate Layer from the Layers palette menu, in the Duplicate Layer dialog box choose the *04Work.psd* file from the Document pop-up menu in the Destination box, and click OK.

3 Make sure the Stopper layer is above the Bottle layer in the Layers palette for the *04Work.psd* file.

4 With the move tool selected, hold down the Shift key, and drag the stopper image up in the document window to position it with its widest edge just above the top of the bottle as shown in the illustration below.

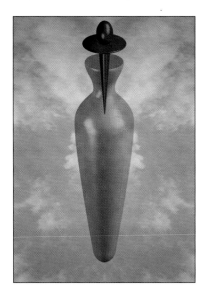

5 Save the *04Work.psd* file.

Copying the Stopper layer

To make the portion of the stopper inside the bottle seem to appear through the glass, you will duplicate the Stopper layer, edit the duplicate Stopper layer, and adjust the opacity and mode of the original Stopper layer.

1 With the Stopper layer selected in the Layers palette for the *04Work.psd* file, choose Duplicate Layer from the Layers palette menu, in the Duplicate Layer dialog box choose the *04Work.psd* file from the Document pop-up menu in the Destination box, and click OK.

The Layers palette displays the Stopper layer copy above the Stopper layer.

CREATING A LAYER MASK

It is also possible to attach a layer mask, a single 8-bit mask channel, to any layer. A layer mask is a viewing option that lets you apply effects to a layer, vary the opacity of a layer, and use channel calculation commands on a layer without destroying layer data.

After editing a layer mask using any of the painting or editing tools, which does not actually manipulate the color values on the layer itself, you will apply the layer mask, which does permanently change the color values on the layer itself.

Note: You can have one layer mask per layer.

Adding a layer mask

In this example, you will create and apply a layer mask to the Stopper layer copy, which will erase the parts of the stopper image below the edge of the bottle.

1 Make sure the Stopper layer is hidden (eye icon not visible) and the Bottle layer is displayed.

2 With the Stopper layer copy selected in the Layers palette, choose Add Layer Mask from the Layers palette menu.

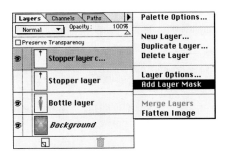

The Layers palette displays a mask thumbnail to the right of the layer thumbnail for the Stopper layer copy. The dark outline around the mask thumbnail indicates it is selected as the current target for any editing or pasting on the layer.

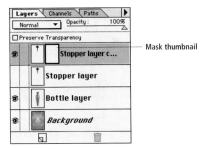

The view of the Stopper layer copy in the document window remains unchanged because the empty layer mask is not masking any portion of the stopper image.

Note: Click either the layer thumbnail or the mask thumbnail to select a current target for a layer.

3 Click the paintbrush tool.

4 In the Brushes palette choose New Brush from the pop-up menu, in the New Brush dialog box enter **13** pixels in the Diameter box, make sure Hardness is set to 0%, and click OK.

5 Magnify the view of the stopper image.

TIP: TO MOVE A SELECTION WITHOUT MOVING PIXELS, HOLD DOWN THE OPTION KEY (OR ALT KEY) AND THE COMMAND KEY (OR CTRL KEY), AND DRAG THE SELECTION TO THE DESIRED POSITION.

6 With the foreground color set to black, and with the layer mask selected as the target (indicated by a dark outline around the mask thumbnail in the Layers palette), paint a mask over the portion of the stopper that is inside the bottle.

Even though it seems as if the stopper is being erased, the original pixels on the layer re-main intact until you apply the layer mask. Also, the mask thumbnail in the Layers palette displays a view of the layer mask.

Note: *Set the foreground color to white to erase portions of the layer mask with the paintbrush. Painting with gray makes areas on the layer partially visible.*

Viewing the mask channel

Although you can see the effect of the mask, by default, the document window does not display the mask channel when you edit the layer mask. When you choose to view and edit the mask channel in the document window, it is also possible to hide or display the layer data.

1 Hold down the Option key (or Alt key), and click the mask thumbnail in the Layers palette.

The document window displays only the mask, and the Layers palette displays the eye icons as dimmed, because you are not seeing any of the layers.

2 In the Layers palette click an eye icon.

The document window displays the layers.

3 Hold down the Shift key, and click the mask thumbnail in the Layers palette.

The document window displays the mask channel on top of the layer in the default masking color.

Note: *It is possible to customize the masking color in the Layer Mask Options dialog box.*

4 Hold down the Shift key, and click the mask thumbnail in the Layers palette.

The document window displays the layers, and the mask channel is hidden.

Applying a layer mask

As you edit a layer mask, all original pixels on the layer remain intact until you apply the layer mask.

1 With the Stopper layer copy still selected in the Layers palette, choose Remove Layer Mask from the Layers palette menu, and when prompted, click Apply to apply the layer mask.

The mask thumbnail is no longer displayed in the Layers palette, and changes to the layer are now permanent.

Note: *After removing a layer mask, it is possible to add another layer mask to the same layer.*

2 With all layers displayed (all eye icons visible), double-click the hand tool to restore the full view of the document.

3 In the Layers palette select the Stopper layer, choose Multiply from the Mode pop-up menu, and set the Opacity slider to 40%.

Even though the stopper image is in front of the bottle image, it seems as if it is visible through the glass bottle.

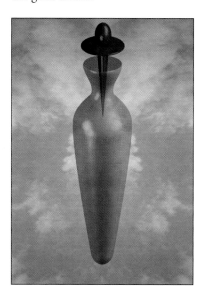

4 Save the *04Work.psd* file.

Creating the label image

After positioning an elliptical selection on the bottle image, you will float the selection and make a layer from the Floating Selection. The correct dimensions for the ellipse are provided.

1 Select the Bottle layer in the Layers palette.

2 Double-click the marquee tool, in the Marquee Options palette choose Elliptical from the Shape pop-up menu and Fixed Size from the Style pop-up menu, and then enter **95** pixels in the Width box and **165** pixels in the Height box.

Note: Hold down the Option key (or Alt key) and click the marquee tool to toggle between the rectangular shape and the elliptical shape.

3 Click the document window, hold down the mouse button, and drag to center the selection over the bottle.

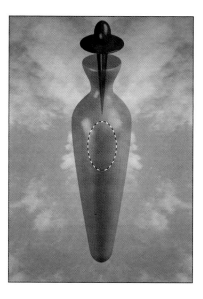

4 With the Bottle layer selected in the Layers palette, float the selection.

The Layers palette displays a Floating Selection above the Bottle layer.

Note: A Floating Selection is defloated (applied to the underlying layer) if you select anything other than the floating selection itself.

5 Drag the Floating Selection to the New Layer icon in the bottom-left corner of the Layers palette, in the Make Layer dialog box type **Label layer** in the Name box, and click OK.

6 Hide all layers except the Label layer.

Placing the label type

1 Make sure the foreground color is set to black and the Label layer is selected in the Layers palette.

2 Select the type tool, click the center of the ellipse, in the Type Tool dialog box choose AGaramond Semibold from the Font pop-up menu, enter **65** points in the Size box, type a lowercase **k** in the text box, and click OK.

3 To precisely center the type in the ellipse, hide the edges of the selection, and press the arrow keys to move the selection in one-pixel increments.

Embossing the label image

After selecting the label, you will apply the Emboss filter. The Emboss filter makes a selection (or an entire layer) appear raised or stamped by suppressing the color within the selection and tracing its edges with black.

1 With the Label layer selected in the Layers palette, choose Stylize from the Filter menu and Emboss from the submenu, in the Emboss dialog box position the cursor over the Preview window, drag to center the image in the Preview window, click the plus button to magnify the view of the label, enter **137** degrees in the Angle box, **6** pixels in the Height box, and **100**% in the Amount box, and click OK.

Colorizing the label image

In addition to colorizing the label image, you will just how easy it is to save the color correction settings. You will also adjust the mode and opacity for the Label layer.

1 Make sure the Label layer is selected in the Layers palette.

2 Choose Adjust from the Image menu and Hue/Saturation from the submenu, in the Hue/Saturation dialog box click the Colorize box, enter **-121** for the Hue and **35** for the Saturation, and click the Save button.

Note: The Colorize option lets you adjust the hue and saturation to fixed values.

3 When prompted, make sure *Projects* is open (selected in the pop-up menu), and type **04SetA.hss** to name the file, and click Save (or OK).

4 In the Hue/Saturation dialog box click OK to apply the settings.

5 With the Label layer selected in the Layers palette, choose Hard Light from the Mode pop-up menu, and adjust the Opacity slider to 80%.

The Hard Light mode gives the effect of shining a harsh spotlight on the image.

6 Make sure all layers are displayed in the document window.

7 Deselect the label image, and save the *04Work.psd* file.

Placing the wing image

After selecting the wing image with the lasso tool in the *04Lib.psd* file, you will drag the selection to the document window of the *04Work.psd* file.

1 With the Label layer selected in the Layers palette of the *04Work.psd* file and with the *04Lib.psd* file active, select the Wings layer in the Layers palette, and make sure all other layers are hidden.

You will use the lasso tool to make a freehand selection of the wing. While it is possible to make a more precise selection using the pen tool, the lasso tool will give a slightly irregular, more interesting edge to the wing.

2 Double-click the lasso tool, and in the Lasso Options palette type **20 pixels** in the Feather Radius box to define a feather edge for the wing.

3 Using the lasso tool, roughly select the wing in the document window.

4 Drag the selection to the *04Work.psd* document window, roughly centering it.

The Layers palette for the *04Work.psd* file displays a Floating Selection above the Label layer.

Note: Like copying and pasting a selection from one file to another file, dragging a selection from the document window of a source file to the document window of a target file automatically adds a Floating Selection to the Layers palette of the target file.

5 In the Layers palette drag the Floating Selection to the New Layer icon in the bottom-left corner, in the Make Layer dialog box type **Wings layer** in the Name box, and click OK.

The Layers palette displays the Wings layer above the Label layer.

Scaling the wing image

You will use the Scale command to reduce the size of the wing.

1 Make sure the Info palette is open, and choose Effects from the Image menu and Scale from the submenu.

Note: The Info palette displays information on the selected tool and on the color values beneath the cursor. Depending on the tool, you can use the Info palette to measure size, distance, and angle of rotation.

2 Hold down the Shift key (to maintain the selection's height-to-width ratio) and drag the bottom-left handle up and right as you watch the height and width percentage in the bottom of the Info palette change to about 55%.

3 Click the gavel icon to confirm the scale.

4 With the move tool selected, drag the wing image to position it to slightly overlap the upper-right side of the bottle.

Rotating the wing image

1 Make sure the Info window is open.

2 Choose Rotate from the Image menu and Free from the submenu, and drag a handle in a clockwise direction until the Info window indicates an angle change of 7°.

3 Click the gavel icon to confirm the scale.

4 If necessary, drag to adjust the position of the wing image.

Colorizing the wing image

You will load stored color correction settings to colorize the wing.

1 Choose Adjust from the Image menu and Hue/Saturation from the submenu, and in the Hue/Saturation dialog box click the Load button.

2 When prompted, select the *04SetB.hss* file in *04Project,* and click the Open button.

3 In the Hue/Saturation dialog box click OK to apply the color correction settings.

WINDOWS PLATFORM:
RENAME ALL *.HSS
FILES TO *.AHU.
RENAME ALL *.CRV
FILES TO *.ACV.

DUPLICATING THE WING IMAGE

After selecting the wing image, you will flip and position the duplicate wing.

1 With the Wings layer selected in the Layers palette, choose Load Selection from the Select menu, in the Load Selection dialog box make sure Wings layer transparency is selected in the Channel pop-up menu, and click OK.

2 Hold down the Option key (or Alt key) and the Shift key (to constrain the movement to 45°) as you drag to the left, away from the wing to duplicate it.

3 Choose Flip from the Image menu and Horizontal from the submenu, and position the flipped wing on the upper-left side of the bottle.

4 Deselect the wing image.

5 With the Wings layer selected, adjust the Opacity slider in the Layers palette to the 70% setting.

6 Make sure all layers are visible, and save the *04Work.psd* file.

Adding a layer mask

You will add and apply a layer mask so that the sections of the wings that overlap the shoulders of the bottle are eliminated.

1 With all layers visible, make sure the Wings layer is selected in the Layers palette.

2 Choose Add Layer Mask from the Layers palette menu.

The Layers palette displays a mask thumbnail to the right of the layer thumbnail for the Stopper layer copy.

Note: Click either the layer thumbnail or the mask thumbnail to select a current target for a layer.

3 Click the paintbrush tool.

4 Make sure the 13-pixel, soft-edged brush is selected in the Brushes palette.

5 Zoom in on the shoulders of the bottle.

6 With the default foreground color set to black, and with the layer mask selected as the target (indicated by a dark outline around the mask thumbnail in the Layers palette), paint a mask over the sections of the wings that overlap the bottle.

Note: Set the foreground color to white to erase portions of the layer mask with the paintbrush.

Applying a layer mask

As you edit a layer mask, all original pixels on the layer remain intact until you apply the layer mask.

1 With the Wings layer still selected in the Layers palette, choose Remove Layer Mask from the Layers palette menu, and when prompted, click Apply to apply the layer mask.

The mask thumbnail is no longer displayed in the Layers palette, and changes to the layer are now permanent.

2 With all layers displayed (all eye icons visible), double-click the hand tool to restore the full view of the document.

Placing the ribbon image

To copy the ribbon image from the *04Lib.psd* file to the *04Work.psd* file you will use the Duplicate Layer command.

1 With the *04Lib.psd* file active, deselect all selections, and select the Ribbon layer in the Layers palette.

2 Choose Duplicate Layer from the Layers palette menu, in the Duplicate Layer dialog box choose the *04Work.psd* file from the Document pop-up menu in the Destination box, and click OK.

The Layers palette for the *04Work.psd* file displays the Ribbon layer.

TIP: TO LINK OR UNLINK
MULTIPLE LAYERS, DRAG
THE CURSOR THROUGH
THE LINK COLUMN IN
THE LAYERS PALETTE.

3 With the move tool selected, hold down the Shift key (to constrain the movement to 45°), and drag to position the ribbon image so that it is about ¾ inch above the bottom of the bottle as shown in the illustration below.

4 With the Ribbon layer selected in the Layers palette, adjust the Opacity slider in the Layers palette to the 70% setting.

Airbrushing a drop shadow

You will paint a drop shadow behind the ribbon that will appear on the bottle.

1 Double-click the airbrush tool, in the Airbrush Options palette choose Behind from the Mode pop-up menu, and set the Pressure slider to 20%.

2 In the Brushes palette select the 100-pixel, soft-edged brush.

3 Paint the bottom edge of the ribbon image just over the bottle image.

Moving linked layers

Depending on how you positioned the various elements in your working document, you may wish to make some final adjustments. In our example, it would improve the overall design if we move all images closer to the bottom edge of the work canvas.

You can use the Layers palette to link layers so that they can be moved as one unit. For this exercise, you will link six layers and drag them together in the document.

1 Make sure the Ribbon layer is selected in the Layers palette.

2 In the Layers palette click the second column from the left for the Wings layer to link it to the Ribbon layer.

The Layers palette displays a link icon in the second column from the left.

3 In the Layers palette continue clicking the second column of the remaining layers to link them together, without including the Background layer.

The link icons in the Layers palette indicate the six linked layers.

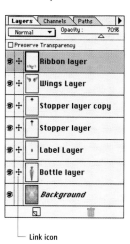

Link icon

4 With the move tool selected, hold down the Shift key (to constrain movement to 45º), and drag up or down in the document window to adjust the position of the linked image to be equally spaced from the top and bottom of the work canvas.

5 In the Layers palette, click the link icons to unlink the layers.

6 Save the *04Work.psd* document.

7 Close open files, and quit (or exit) the Adobe Photoshop application.

KENYA

5

We wanted an inviting and unexpected approach to this exhibition
poster while still allowing the pieces
in this collection of African acces-
sories to speak for themselves. ■ The
typeface featured in this poster is

ART EXHIBITION POSTER

Lithos, an Adobe Originals typeface
designed by Carol Twombly in 1989.
Extremely popular since its release,
the flexible design of this typeface
combines simplified character shapes
with a playful asymmetric quality
that works well for a large variety of
display jobs. The inspiration for
Lithos comes from ancient Greeks
who honored public figures by chis-
eling geometric letterforms, free of
adornment, into stone. These inscrip-
tions served to honor public figures
or as dedications for temples.

To create this poster, you will draw, edit, and use effects and filters on different layers, to experiment with different combinations and placements of graphics, type, and special effects without discarding image data, until the desired effect is

ART EXHIBITION POSTER

achieved. You will also add and edit a layer mask without affecting pixels in the underlying layer. In addition to adding a layer mask, you will also group two layers into a clipping group. In a clipping group, the bottom layer in the group controls the mode and transparency for all other layers in the group, so that all the layers clip to the base layer. Using this technique, it is possible to fill the type with the pattern with great ease.

This project also covers:

• Converting CMYK color images to bitmap mode

• Resizing a document using the Canvas Size command

• Rotating an image

• Applying color gradient fills to an image

• Creating a layer mask

• Applying the Add Noise filter

• Placing images by dragging a layer

• Creating a precision drop shadow

• Defining a pattern

• Creating a clipping group.

It should take you about 2 hours to complete this project.

Viewing the final image

1 Before launching the Adobe Photoshop application, throw away the Adobe Photoshop Preferences file to ensure all settings are returned to their default values.

2 Make sure the Lithos font, found on the *Advanced Adobe Photoshop* CD-ROM disc, is installed.

3 Launch the Adobe Photoshop application, and open the *05Final.psd* file in *05Project* to view the final image.

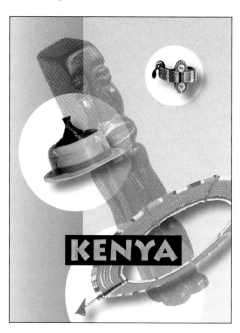

4 Reduce the view of the *05Final.psd* document, and drag it to the upper-right corner of your desktop to use as a visual reference.

CREATING THE STATUE IMAGE

After opening the statue image and converting it from CMYK mode to Grayscale mode to Bitmap mode, you will resize the canvas, and then colorize and rotate the entire image.

Opening an Adobe Photoshop file

Rather than creating a new file, you will open the existing Adobe Photoshop file, *Statue.psd*.

1 Open the *Statue.psd* file in *05Project*.

The statue image was scanned from a 2¼ inch transparency on a Leafscan 45 transparency scanner at a resolution of 300 dpi. For the sake of reducing the demand for disk space on your system, you will use a working file with a resolution of 72 dpi.

Converting the image from CMYK to Bitmap mode

Bitmap images consist of one bit of color (black or white) per pixel and require the least amount of memory of all image types. To convert an CMYK color image to a bitmapped image, you must first convert it to a grayscale image.

1 Choose Grayscale from the Mode menu, and when you are prompted to discard the color information, click OK.

The hue and saturation information from the pixels is removed, leaving the brightness information.

2 Choose Bitmap from the Mode menu, in the Bitmap dialog box make sure the Output box is set to 72 pixels/inch, choose the Halftone Screen option in the Method box, and click OK to convert the grayscale image to a bitmapped image.

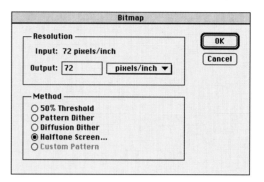

The Halftone Screen option simulates the effect of printing a grayscale image through a halftone screen.

3 In the Halftone Screen dialog box enter **12** lines/inch, make sure the Angle is set to 45°, choose Round from the Shape pop-up menu, and click OK.

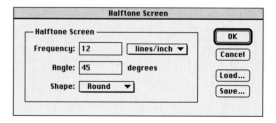

4 Save the *Statue.psd* file as *05Work.psd* to *Projects*.

Colorizing the statue image

To colorize the statue image, you must convert the bitmapped image to a color mode. It is not possible to convert directly from bitmapped to CMYK. You must begin by converting the bitmapped image to a grayscale image, so that you can convert the grayscale image to CMYK color mode, and then you can colorize the image.

1 Choose Grayscale from the Mode menu, in the Grayscale dialog box make sure the Size Ratio is set to 1, and click OK.

2 Choose CMYK Color from the Mode menu.

The color values for each pixel are assigned that pixel's previous gray value.

3 Choose All from the Select menu.

4 Click the foreground color swatch in the toolbox, and in the Color Picker dialog box enter the following settings:

> Cyan...............61
> Magenta.........31
> Yellow..............0
> Black 1

5 Click OK to set the foreground color to blue.

6 Choose Fill from the Edit menu, in the Fill dialog box choose Lighten from the Mode pop-up menu, and click OK.

In Lighten mode, the Adobe Photoshop application looks at the color information and selects the lighter of the base or blend color. Pixels darker than the blend color are replaced, and pixels lighter than the blend color do not change.

Resizing the canvas

The Canvas Size command allows you to add work space, or extra canvas area, around an existing image without changing the dimensions of the image.

Note: You can use the Canvas Size command to crop an image; however, if you want to adjust the size and resolution of an image, you should use the Image Size command or the cropping tool.

1 Choose Canvas Size from the Image menu, in the Canvas Size dialog box enter **6** inches in the Width box in the New Size box and make sure the Height is set to 8 inches, make sure the Placement option is set to be centered, and click OK.

Rotating the statue image

1 Select the entire contents of the Background layer.

2 Choose Rotate from the Image menu and Arbitrary from the submenu, in the Arbitrary Rotate dialog box enter **30°** in the Angle box, click the CCW (counterclockwise) option, and click OK.

3 Deselect the statue, and save the *05Work.psd* file.

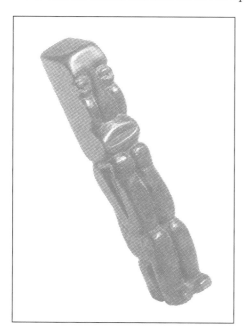

APPLYING A COLOR GRADIENT FILL

To demonstrate how much freedom and flexibility image processing on layers can provide, you will fill the left side of the vertical split with purple (not the rose color shown in the final image). Later in the project you will fill the left side with the rose color.

1 In the Layers palette click the New Layer icon in the lower-left corner, in the New Layer dialog box type **Gradient color layer** in the Name box, and click OK.

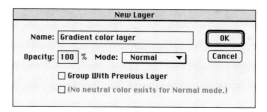

2 With the Gradient color layer selected in the Layers palette and with the rectangular marquee tool selected and set to Normal, drag in the document window to select the right two-thirds of the work canvas as shown in the illustration below.

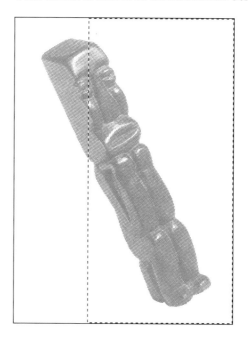

3 Click the foreground color swatch in the toolbox, and in the Color Picker dialog box enter the following settings:

Cyan..............23
Magenta...........0
Yellow.............93
Black 0

4 Click OK to set the foreground color to yellow.

5 Click the background color swatch in the toolbox, and in the Color Picker dialog box enter the following settings:

Cyan.................6
Magenta...........0
Yellow.............27
Black 0

6 Click OK to set the background color to light yellow.

7 With the gradient tool selected and with the right side still selected, drag from the top-left corner of the selection to the lower-right corner to apply the gradient.

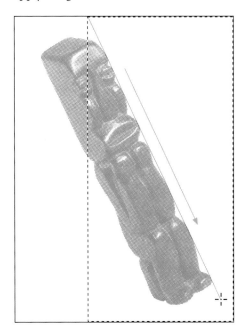

8 In the Layers palette double-click the Gradient color layer, in the Layer Options dialog box choose Multiply from the Mode pop-up menu, and click OK.

In Multiply mode, painting over an area multiplies the color values and darkens the image. The effect is similar to drawing on the image with multiple magic markers.

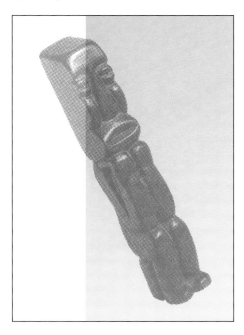

9 Inverse the selection to select the left side of the work canvas.

10 Click the foreground color swatch in the toolbox, and in the Color Picker dialog box enter the following settings:

Cyan 56
Magenta 24
Yellow 0
Black................ 1

11 Click OK to set the foreground color to purple.

12 Click the background color swatch in the toolbox, and in the Color Picker dialog box enter the following settings:

Cyan...............19
Magenta.........21
Yellow...............0
Black 0

13 Click OK to set the background color to a light purple.

14 To apply a gradient fill to the selection, drag from the center of the right edge of the selection directly across to the center of the left edge.

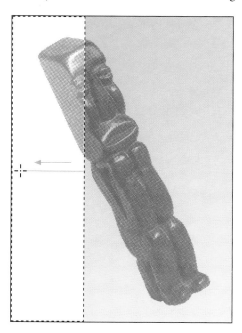

15 Choose Save Selection from the Select menu, and in the Save Selection dialog box click OK.

The Channels palette displays alpha channel #5. With this selection saved in an alpha channel, it will be easy to select it again to be re-colorized to rose as shown in the final image.

16 Save the *05Work.psd* file.

ADDING A LAYER MASK

You will add and edit a layer mask on the Gradient color layer using the gradient tool.

A layer mask is a viewing option that lets you experiment with revealing parts of a layer, without actually altering the pixel information on the layer itself.

1 With the Gradient color layer selected in the Layers palette, choose Add Layer Mask from the Layers palette menu.

The Gradient color layer in the Layers palette displays a mask thumbnail to the right of the layer thumbnail. The dark outline around the mask thumbnail indicates the layer mask is the target for editing on the Gradient color layer.

Note: Click either the layer thumbnail or the mask thumbnail to select one as the target for editing.

2 Double-click the marquee tool, in the Marquee Options palette choose Elliptical from the Shape pop-up menu, choose Fixed Size from the Style pop-up menu, and enter **114** pixels in the Width box and **114** pixels in the Height box.

3 With the mask thumbnail selected in the Gradient color layer in the Layers palette, click the document window, and drag the circle to the upper-right corner, about ¾ inch from the top and right sides of the work canvas.

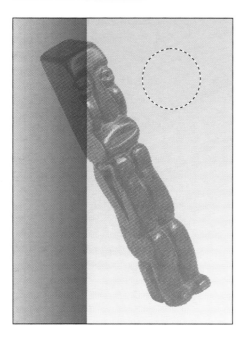

4 Fill the circle with black.

The Layers palette displays a black circle in the mask thumbnail, and the document window displays the Background layer through the masked (or transparent) portions of the Gradient color layer.

5 In the Marquee Options palette enter **222** pixels in the Width box and **222** pixels in the Height box.

6 Click the document window, and drag the circle to the upper-left corner, about 2 inches from the top edge of the work canvas and about ¼ inch from the left side.

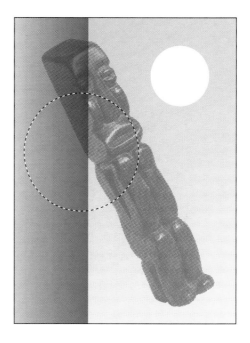

7 Fill the circle with black.

8 In the Marquee Options palette enter **270** pixels in the Width box and **270** pixels in the Height box.

9 Click the document window, and drag the circle so that the circle is about 1½ inches from the left edge of the work canvas and about three-fourths of the circle is above the bottom edge of the work canvas.

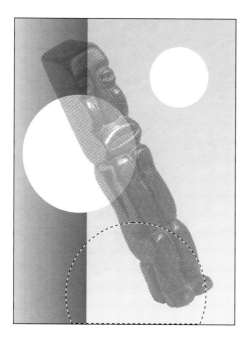

10 Fill the circle with black.

Editing the layer mask

To demonstrate how all pixels underlying the layer mask have remained intact, you will select the smallest circle in the layer mask with the marquee tool, and then move the selection anywhere in the document window.

1 In the Marquee Options dialog box choose Rectangular from the Shape pop-up menu and Normal from the Style pop-up menu.

2 With the mask thumbnail selected in the Gradient color layer in the Layers palette, drag a rectangular selection around the smallest circle, and drag it in the document window to any new position.

The document window displays how all underlying pixels have remained intact, and you are free to edit the layer mask without losing color information.

3 Drag the smallest circle to the original suggested position as shown in the final image, and deselect it.

EDITING THE GRADIENT COLOR LAYER

After re-colorizing the purple portion of the Gradient color layer to be rose as shown in the final image, you will apply the Add Noise filter.

Re-colorizing the Gradient color layer

After loading the selection saved in alpha channel #4, you will fill the left side of the vertical divide with a rose color rather than the original purple color.

1 In the Layers palette select the layer thumbnail for the Gradient color layer.

2 Choose Load Selection from the Select menu, in the Load Selection dialog box make sure alpha channel #5 is selected from the Channel pop-up menu, and click OK.

The left portion of the work canvas is selected.

3 Click the foreground color swatch in the tool-box, and in the Color Picker dialog box enter the following settings:

Cyan.................8
Magenta.........85
Yellow.............60
Black 1

4 Click OK to set the foreground color to rose.

5 Click the background color swatch in the tool-box, and in the Color Picker dialog box enter the following settings:

Cyan.................6
Magenta.........23
Yellow.............10
Black 0

6 Click OK to set the background color to light rose.

7 As before, to apply the gradient fill to the selection, drag from the center of the right edge of the selection directly across to the center of the left edge.

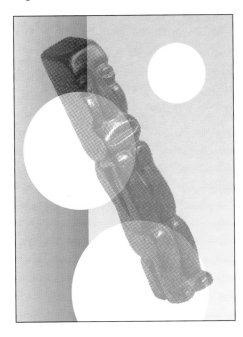

8 Save the *05Work.psd* file.

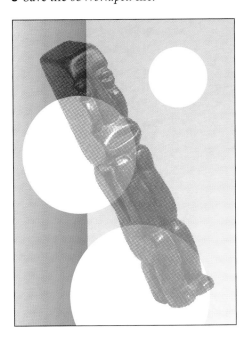

Applying the Add Noise filter

The Add Noise filter applies random pixels to an image, simulating the effect of shooting pictures on high-speed film.

1 With the Gradient color layer selected in the Layers palette, select the entire layer.

Note: To apply the Add Noise filter to an entire layer, select or deselect everything on the target layer.

1 Choose Noise from the Filter menu and Add Noise from the submenu, in the Add Noise dialog box enter **20** in the Amount box, and click OK.

The value you specify in the Amount box is used as the standard deviation of the color values of the noise.

PLACING THE IMAGES

The *05Lib.psd* file is a library of images, consisting of three images on three separate layers. To place these images into the *05Work.psd* file you will drag the appropriate layer from the Layers palette of the *05Lib.psd* file to the document window of the *05Work.psd* file, automatically adding a layer to the *05Work.psd* file. Once all three images are placed in the *05Work.psd* file, you will merge the three layers into one layer.

Placing the bracelet image

1 Open the *05Lib.psd* file in *05Project*.

2 Drag the Bracelet layer from the Layers palette of the *05Lib.psd file* to the document window of the *05Work.psd* file.

The Layers palette for the *05Work.psd* file displays the Bracelet layer, and the document window displays the bracelet image.

3 With the move tool selected and with the Bracelet layer selected in the Layers palette of the *05Work.psd* file, drag in the document window to position the bracelet image over the upper-right circle.

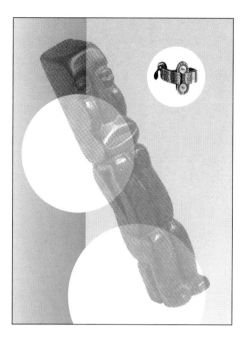

Placing the hat image

1 With the hat image displayed in the document window of the *05Lib.psd* file, drag the Hat layer from the Layers palette of the *05Lib.psd file* to the document window of the *05Work.psd* file.

As before, the Layers palette for the *05Work.psd* file displays the Hat layer and the document window displays the hat image.

2 Make sure the Hat layer is selected in the Layers palette of the *05Work.psd* file.

3 With the move tool selected, drag in the document window to position the hat image over the upper-left circle.

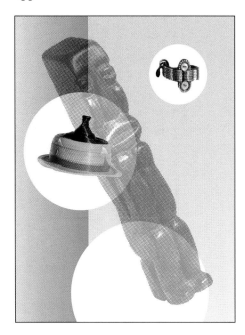

4 Select the entire contents of the Hat layer.

5 Choose Rotate from the Image menu and Arbitrary from the submenu, in the Arbitrary Rotate dialog box enter **30°** in the Angle box, click the CCW (counterclockwise) option, and click OK.

6 Deselect the hat image.

Placing the collar image

1 With the collar image displayed in the document window of the *05Lib.psd* file, drag the Collar layer from the Layers palette of the *05Lib.psd file* to the document window of the *05Work.psd* file.

Again, the Layers palette for the *05Work.psd* file displays the Collar layer and the document window displays the collar image.

2 Make sure the Collar layer is selected in the Layers palette of the *05Work.psd* file.

3 With the move tool selected, drag in the document window to position the collar image in the lower-right corner.

4 Select the entire contents of the Collar layer.

5 Choose Rotate from the Image menu and Arbitrary from the submenu, in the Arbitrary Rotate dialog box enter **45°** in the Angle box, click the CW (clockwise) option, and click OK.

6 With the move tool selected, adjust the position of the collar image if necessary.

7 Deselect the collar image.

8 Save the *05Work.psd* file.

CREATING A PRECISION DROP SHADOW

After merging the three layers you just added to your working document, you will copy the merged layer and then completely desaturate the original merged layer of color to create a precision drop shadow.

Merging the layers

When you are experimenting in layers, it's a good idea to work with individual elements on separate layers. When you've finalized the characteristics and positioning of the layer contents, you can merge one or more layers to create intermediate versions of your composite image. In addition, merging keeps your file size manageable, especially when you are working in large documents.

You will merge three layers into a single layer using the Merge Layers command. When you use the Merge Layers command, only the layers that are displayed in the document window (eye icons visible in the Layers palette) are merged into a single layer. All undisplayed layers remain intact.

Note: One of the layers to be merged must be selected (highlighted) in the Layers palette to activate the Merge Layers command in the Layers palette menu.

1 In the Layers palette of the *05Work.psd* file make sure the Bracelet layer, the Hat layer, and the Collar layer are the only layers displayed (eye icons visible), so that Background layer and the Gradient color layer are not displayed (eye icons not visible).

2 Make sure one of the layers to be merged is selected in the Layers palette.

3 Choose Merge Layers from the Layers palette menu.

The three layers are merged into the bottom-most layer, Bracelet layer.

4 In the Layers palette double-click the Bracelet layer, in the Layer Options dialog box type **Jewelry layer** in the Name box, and click OK.

5 In the Layers palette make sure all layers are displayed.

Copying the Jewelry layer

You will make a copy of the Jewelry layer, and then you will edit the original Jewelry layer using the Desaturate command and the Threshold command to create a drop shadow.

The Threshold command allows you to convert grayscale or color images to high-contrast black-and-white images. This command enables you to specify a certain level as a threshold. All pixels lighter than the threshold are converted to white. All pixels darker than the threshold are converted to black.

The Desaturate command allows you to change the saturation of all colors to 0, that is, to convert all colors to their grayscale equivalent. This command enables you to quickly convert colors to gray without changing modes.

1 In the Layers palette drag the Jewelry layer to the New Layer icon.

The Layers palette displays the newly created Jewelry layer copy.

2 In the Layers palette click the eye icon to hide the Jewelry layer copy, and select the (original) Jewelry layer to be the target layer.

3 Choose Adjust from the Image menu and Desaturate from the submenu.

4 Choose Map from the Image menu and Threshold from the submenu, in the Threshold dialog box activate the Preview option, enter **255** in the Threshold Level box, and click OK.

5 Choose Blur from the Filter menu and Gaussian Blur from the submenu, in the Gaussian Blur dialog box enter **8** pixels in the Amount box, and click OK.

6 With the Jewelry layer selected in the Layers palette, set the Opacity setting to 50%.

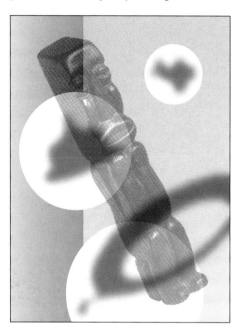

7 To offset the shadow, make sure the Jewelry layer is selected in the Layers palette, select the move tool, and drag in the document window to position the entire image about ¼ inch down and right.

8 Make sure all layers are displayed (eye icons visible) to view the results, and save the *05Work.psd* file.

MERGING THE LAYERS

You will merge all layers into the Background layer using the Merge Layers command. Although it is possible to use the Flatten Image command to merge all layers, as a rule of thumb, you may wish to use the Flatten Image command with discretion since any undisplayed layers are discarded.

1 With all layers are displayed, make sure one of the layers is selected in the Layers palette.

2 Choose Merge Layers from the Layers palette menu.

The Layers palette displays the Background layer.

CREATING THE PATTERNED TYPE

After creating the black box on its own layer, placing type on its own layer, and creating a pattern on its own layer, you will specify the Type layer and the Pattern layer to be a clipping group, allowing the pattern to be clipped to the type as shown in the final image.

Creating the black box

1 In the Layers palette click the New Layer icon, in the New Layer dialog box type **Box layer** in the Name box, and click OK.

2 Double-click the marquee tool, in the Marquee Options palette make sure Rectangular is selected in the Shape pop-up menu and Fixed Size is selected in the Style pop-up menu, and enter **227** pixels in the Width box and **57** pixels in the Height box.

3 Drag to center the box about 2 inches above the bottom edge of the document.

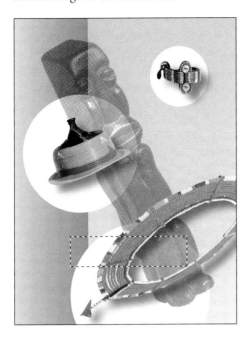

4 Fill the box with black.

5 Deselect the box.

Placing the KENYA type

After positioning the type over the black box, you will create a pattern on its own layer.

1 In the Layers palette click the New Layer icon, in the New Layer dialog box type **Type layer** in the Name box, and click OK.

2 Make sure the foreground color is set to black.

3 Select the type tool, click the black box in the document window, in the Type Tool dialog box choose Lithos Black from the Font pop-up menu, enter **55** points in the Size pop-up menu, type **KENYA** in uppercase letters in the text box, and click OK.

4 With the move tool selected, drag to center the selected type in the black box.

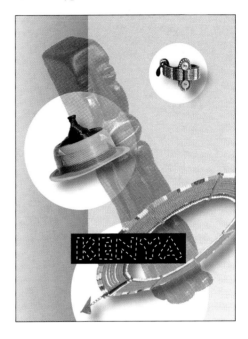

5 Deselect the type, and save the *05Work.psd* file.

DEFINING A PATTERN

After creating a pattern using the Define Pattern command, you will use the Fill command to fill a rectangular-shaped selection with the pattern.

1 In the Layers palette click the eye icon to hide the Type layer.

2 In the Layers palette click the New Layer icon, in the New Layer dialog box type **Pattern layer** in the Name box, and click OK.

3 Double-click the marquee tool, and in the Marquee Options dialog box make sure Rectangle is selected from the Shape pop-up menu and Normal is selected from the Style pop-up menu.

4 With the Background layer selected in the Layers palette, drag to select a portion of the hat that contains roughly equal parts of orange and blue as shown in the illustration below.

5 Choose Define Pattern from the Edit menu.

6 Deselect the portion of the hat.

7 With the Pattern layer selected in the Layers palette, choose Fill from the Edit menu, in the Fill dialog box choose Pattern from the Contents pop-up menu, choose Normal from the Mode pop-up menu, and click OK.

The entire layer is filled with the pattern.

CREATING A CLIPPING GROUP

Working with a group of layers as a single unit allows you to maintain great flexibility in designing an image. In a clipping group, the bottom layer (or base layer) in the group controls the mode and transparency for all the other layer in the group. In effect, all the layers "clip" to the base layer.

In this example you will group the Pattern layer and the Type layer. Since the Type layer is the base layer, the pattern will be masked to the opaque areas (the type itself) on the Type layer.

Note: *When you have the effect you want, you can merge the clipping group into the base layer.*

1 To group the Pattern layer and the Type layer, hold down the Option key (or Alt key), position the cursor over the solid divider line between the Pattern layer and the Type layer in the Layers palette until the cursor is displayed as the grouping icon, and click the line.

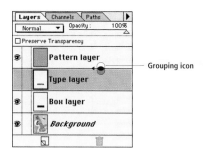

Note: To remove a layer from a group, hold down the Option key (or Alt key) and click the dotted divider line.

2 Make sure all layers are visible to view the final result.

3 Save the *05Work.psd* file.

PRINTING A POSTER

In this example, for the sake of reducing the demand for disk space on your system, you have worked with a file whose dimensions are 6 inches by 8 inches with a resolution of 72 pixels per inch (ppi).

To print a poster, it would be necessary to establish your Adobe Photoshop file size to equal the final printing size. In this case, the exhibition poster is meant to be 18 inches by 24 inches. To determine the optimal resolution of your working file, you must first know the halftone screen frequency at which you will be printing. For our purposes, 150 lines per inch (lpi) is satisfactory, and so by doubling the lpi value it is possible to compute the optimal resolution of 300 ppi for our working file resolution. For more information on printing, refer to the *Adobe Photoshop User Guide.*

4 Close all files, and quit (or exit) the Adobe Photoshop application.

Hautmont…pour tes cheveux.

6

In this project you will create a billboard for the French cosmetic firm, Hautmont. Their product line includes Hautmont shampoo... pour

BILLBOARD LAYOUT

tes cheveux (for your hair). ■ The model was photographed in front of a green backdrop, so we selected the model image exclusive of the background, and placed the image on its own layer in a library of images. The entire shampoo bottle image (including the type) was created in Adobe Dimensions™, a 3-D design tool, and placed in the library of images as well. As for the rippled water background, you will create it yourself using the Ripple filter that is included in the Adobe Photoshop application.

The Garamond typeface and its variations have been a standard among book designers and printers for four centuries. These original typefaces, based on the types of the sixteenth-century printer, publisher, and type designer Claude Garamond,

BILLBOARD COMPOSITION

were modeled on those of the Venetian printers from the end of the previous century. This project features the first Adobe Originals typeface, Adobe Garamond. Adobe designer Robert Slimbach went to the Plantin-Moretus museum in Antwerp, Belgium, to study the original Garamond typefaces. These typefaces served as the basis for the design of the Adobe Garamond romans; the italics are based on types by Robert Granjon, a contemporary of Garamond's. The elegant, versatile design was released in 1989, and includes three weights, plus a titling font, alternate characters, and an Expert Collection to provide a flexible family of typefaces.

This project covers:

- Creating a color gradient fill

- Applying the Ripple filter

- Adding a layer mask

- Copying a path from one file to another.

It should take you about 90 minutes to complete this project.

Viewing the final image

Before you begin to create the billboard, take a moment to view the final image.

1 Before you launch the Adobe Photoshop application, throw away the Adobe Photoshop Preferences file to make sure all settings are returned to their default values.

2 Make sure the Adobe Garamond font, found on the *Advanced Adobe Photoshop* CD-ROM disc, is installed.

3 Launch the Adobe Photoshop application, and open the *06Final.psd* file in *06Project* to view the final image.

Hautmont...pour tes cheveux.

4 Reduce the view of the *06Final.psd* document, and drag it to the upper-right corner of your desktop to use as a visual reference.

Opening a new document

1 Create a new file, and in the New dialog box enter **06Work.psd** in the Name box, **540** pixels in the Width box, **345** pixels in the Height box, and **100** pixels per inch in the Resolution box, choose CMYK color from the Mode menu, and click OK.

2 Save the *06Work.psd* file to *Projects*.

CREATING THE RIPPLED BACKGROUND

After applying a blue gradient fill to the background, you will paint white lines on the gradient fill, and then apply the Ripple filter to distort the image.

Time out for a movie

If your system is capable of running Adobe Teach movies, you can see a preview of the technique used to create the rippled background that is covered in this section. Play the movie named Ripple Filter. For information on how to play Adobe Teach movies, see the "What You Need To Do" section at the beginning of this book.

TIP: HOLD DOWN THE OPTION KEY (OR ALT KEY) AND PRESS THE DELETE KEY TO FILL A SELECTION WITH THE FOREGROUND COLOR.

Applying the color gradient fill

The gradient tool lets you create a gradient fill, displaying a gradual transition from the foreground color to the background color.

1 Choose Show Rulers from the Window menu to display the rulers.

2 With the marquee tool selected, drag to create a rectangle, approximately 2 inches high by 3 inches wide in the upper-left corner of the document as shown in the illustration below.

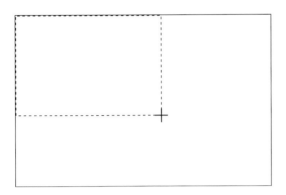

3 With the Picker palette open, choose CMYK sliders from the Picker palette menu, and set the values as follows:

> Cyan...........88%
> Magenta.....17%
> Yellow.........12%
> Black............4%

4 Make sure the background color is set to white.

You will drag the gradient just beyond the lower-right corner to ensure the lower-right corner contains a trace of the azure blue color.

5 Now that the foreground color is set to azure blue, double-click the gradient tool, in the Gradient Tool Options palette make sure Foreground to Background is selected from the Style pop-up

menu, and drag from the upper-left corner to about ⅛ inch beyond the lower-right corner of the selection as shown in the illustration below.

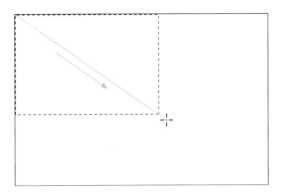

Applying the Ripple filter

The Ripple filter produces an undulating pattern on a selection, like ripples on the surface of a pond. Before you apply the Ripple filter, you will paint the white lines on the gradient fill.

1 With the foreground color set to white, click the paintbrush tool, and in the Brushes palette select the 13-pixel, soft-edged brush (third from the left, second row).

2 Paint a double-x mark as shown in the illustration below.

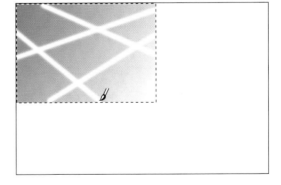

3 Choose Distort from the Filter menu and Ripple from the submenu, in the Ripple dialog box enter **600** in the Amount box, set the Size of the ripple frequency to Large, and click OK.

4 Choose Effects from the Image menu and Scale from the submenu, and drag the lower-right handle to the lower-right corner of the document as shown in the illustration below.

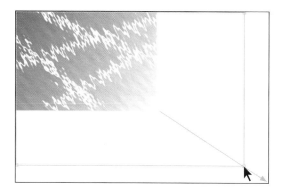

Scaling the image to be larger produces a slightly softened effect.

5 Click the gavel icon to confirm the scale.

PLACING IMAGES AND TYPE

In addition to placing images and type, you will copy paths from the *06Lib.psd* file to your working document. In addition, you will add and edit a layer mask, and then experiment with moving the layer and the layer mask in unison and independently.

Placing the bottle image

You will drag the Bottle layer from the *06Lib.psd* file to the *06Work.psd* file, and then rotate and position the bottle image.

1 Open the *06Lib.psd* file in *06Project*.

2 In the Layers palette hide the Model layer (eye icon not visible), and make sure the Bottle layer is displayed.

3 Drag the Bottle layer from the Layers palette of the *06Lib.psd* file to the document window of the *06Work.psd* file.

The Layers palette of the *06Work.psd* file displays the Bottle layer, and the document window displays the bottle image at the point where you released the mouse button.

4 Select the entire image on the Bottle layer.

5 Choose Rotate from the Image menu and Arbitrary from the submenu, in the Arbitrary Rotate dialog box enter **52°** in the Angle box, make sure the CW (clockwise) option is selected, and click OK.

6 With the move tool selected, drag in the document window to position the bottle image in the upper-right corner of the work canvas.

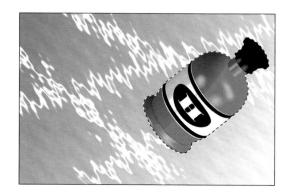

7 Deselect the bottle image.

Adding a layer mask

After adding a layer mask to the Bottle layer, you will edit the layer mask using the gradient tool, causing the bottom edge of the bottle image to appear as though it fades into the water.

A layer mask is a viewing option that lets you experiment with revealing parts of a layer, without actually altering the pixel information on the layer itself.

1 With the Bottle layer selected in the Layers palette of the *06Work.psd* file, choose Add Layer Mask from the Layers palette menu.

The Bottle layer in the Layers palette displays a mask thumbnail to the right of the layer thumbnail. The dark outline around the mask thumbnail indicates the layer mask is the target for editing on the Bottle layer.

Note: *Click either the layer thumbnail or the mask thumbnail to select a target for editing.*

2 Make sure the mask thumbnail on the Bottle layer is selected as the target.

3 With the default colors selected, select the gradient tool, drag from about one inch below the bottle to the center of the bottle as shown in the illustration below, and release the mouse button.

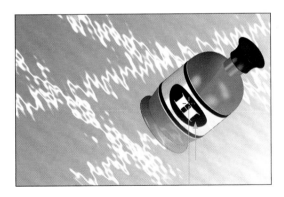

The mask thumbnail in the Layers palette displays the gradient applied to the lower portion of the layer mask.

4 In the Layers palette set the opacity of the Bottle layer to 85%.

5 Save the *06Work.psd* file.

Placing the model image

You will drag the Model layer from the *06Lib.psd* file to the *06Work.psd* file, and then position it.

1 In the Layers palette select the layer thumbnail for the Bottle layer.

2 Make sure the *06Lib.psd* file is open.

3 In the Layers palette select the Model layer and hide the Bottle layer (eye icon not visible).

4 Drag the Model layer from the Layers palette of the *06Lib.psd* file to the document window of the *06Work.psd* file.

The Layers palette for the *06Work.psd* file displays the Model layer, and the document window displays the model image at the point where you released the mouse button.

5 With the move tool selected, drag in the document window to position the model image about ¼ inch from the top and left edge of the work canvas as shown in the illustration below.

Adding a layer mask

After adding a layer mask to the Model layer, you will edit the layer mask using the gradient tool, causing the right edge of the model image to appear as though it fades into the water.

1 With the Model layer selected in the Layers palette, choose Add Layer Mask from the Layers palette menu.

The Model layer in the Layers palette displays a mask thumbnail to the right of the layer thumbnail.

2 With the default colors selected and with the gradient tool selected, drag from the right edge of the model's hair to the center of her nose, and release the mouse button.

3 Save the *06Work.psd* file.

Placing the curved path

You will copy line art (in the form of a stored path) from the *06Lib.psd* file to the *06Work.psd* file.

1 In the Layers palette click the New Layer icon, in the New Layer dialog box enter **Line art/type layer** in the Name box, and click OK.

2 Open the Paths palette for the *06Lib.psd* file, and drag the Curved lines path from the Paths palette of the *06Lib.psd* file to the document window of the *06Work.psd* file.

The Paths palette for the *06Work.psd* file displays the Curved lines path, and the document window displays the curved lines path as selected.

Note: The path is positioned at the point where you release the mouse. If the path falls outside the window of the document you are copying to, the path is cropped (not clipped). The path is not clipped until you select another path.

3 Make sure the Line art/type layer is selected in the Layers palette, and make sure all layers are displayed (eye icons visible).

4 In the Paths palette click the arrow tool and click the Curved lines path to make sure the path is selected in the document window.

Note: *To select a path, select the arrow tool in the Paths palette, and drag a marquee selection around the path.*

5 Drag in the document window to position the curved lines path above the bottle image.

Stroking the curved path with red

1 With the eyedropper tool selected, click the model's mouth to set the foreground color to red.

2 Click the pencil tool, in the Brushes palette select the 2-pixel, hard-edged brush (second brush in the first row).

The pencil tool creates hard-edged freehand lines, applying its effects along the border of the path.

3 Make sure the Line art/type layer is selected in the Layers palette.

4 In the Paths palette make sure the Curved lines path is selected, and click the Stroke icon at the bottom of the Paths palette, second from the left.

5 In the Paths palette click under the paths to deselect the curved lines path.

Placing the box path

Again, you will copy line art (in the form of a stored path) from the *06Lib.psd* file to the *06Work.psd* file.

1 Drag the Box path from the Paths palette of the *06Lib.psd* file to the document window of the *06Work.psd* file.

The Paths palette for the *06Work.psd* file displays the Box path, and the document window displays the box path as selected.

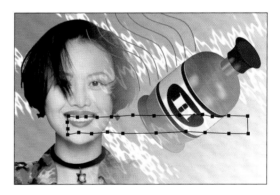

2 Make sure the Line art/type layer is selected in the Layers palette, and make sure all layers are displayed (eye icons visible).

3 In the Paths palette click the Box path to make sure the path is selected in the document window.

4 With the arrow tool selected in the Paths palette, drag in the document window to center the box path about ½ inch from the bottom of the work canvas.

Filling the box path with white

1 Set the foreground color to white.

2 In the Paths palette make sure the Box path is selected, and click the Fill icon in the bottom-left corner of the Paths palette.

3 In the Paths palette click under the paths to deselect the box path.

Airbrushing a drop shadow

You will airbrush a drop shadow around the edge of the white box.

1 Double-click the airbrush tool, in the Airbrush Options palette choose Behind from the Mode pop-up menu, and set the Pressure slider to 9%.

2 In the Brushes palette select the 65-pixel, soft-edged brush.

3 With the foreground color to black, airbrush along the edge of the white box.

Placing the type

You will place the type in the white box.

1 Open the Layers palette.

1 With the Line art/type layer selected in the Layers palette, select the type tool, click the white box, in the Type Tool dialog box choose AGaramond Semibold from the Font pop-up menu, enter **18** points in the Size box, and type **Hautmont…pour tes cheveux.** in the text box, and click OK.

2 Hide the edges of the selected type, select the move tool, and make sure the Line art/type layer is selected in the Layers palette.

3 Drag to center the type in the white box about 1 inch from the right edge of the white box as shown in the illustration below.

4 Deselect the type, and save the *06Work.psd* file.

Placing the small bottle image

After copying the bottle image from the *06Lib.psd* file, you will scale it and position it in the white box.

1 Drag the Bottle layer from the Layers palette in the *06Lib.psd* file to the document window of the *06Work.psd* file.

2 Make sure the entire bottle image is displayed in the document window to prevent cropping.

The Layers palette for the *06Work.psd* file displays two layers named Bottle layer.

3 Double-click the newly added Bottle layer, the upper-most layer in the Layers palette, in the Layer Options dialog box type **Small bottle layer** in the Name box, and click OK.

4 With the Info palette open, choose Effects from the Image menu and Scale from the submenu, hold down the Shift key (to maintain the proportions), and drag a handle until the Info palette indicates the size is reduced to 15%.

5 Click the gavel icon to confirm the scale.

6 With the move tool selected, drag in the document window to position the small bottle image inside the right portion of the white box as shown in the illustration below.

7 Deselect the small bottle.

Airbrushing a drop shadow

You will airbrush a drop shadow for the small bottle.

1 Double-click the airbrush tool, and in the Airbrush Options palette make sure Behind is selected from the Mode pop-up menu and the Pressure slider is set to 9%.

2 In the Brushes palette select a 45-pixel, soft-edged brush.

3 With the Small bottle layer selected in the Layers palette, airbrush the lower-right edge of the small bottle as shown in the illustration below.

4 Save the *06Work.psd* file.

5 Close all files, and quit (or exit) the Adobe Photoshop application.

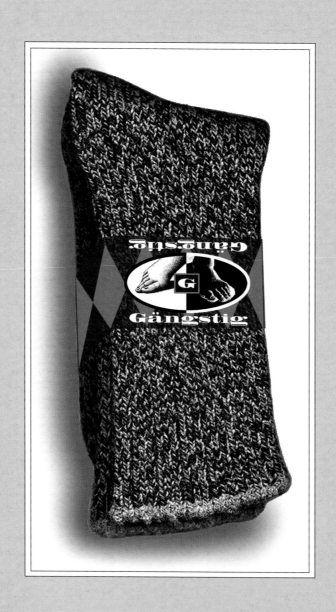

7

Use Adobe Photoshop to create powerful, realistic product packaging mock-ups. With the layering feature, you can organize numerous variations of a design within a single

PACKAGING PRESENTATION

Adobe Photoshop document. When you are ready to present your ideas to a client, open the document, and hide and show different layers to view the possibilities. ■ In this example you will create several color variations and several type variations for a ribbon that wraps around a pair of socks by Gängstig, a Swedish company specializing in outdoor recreation products. We chose the name Gängstig because it means "footpath" in Swedish.

Saving the expense of actually photographing socks, we scanned a real pair of socks on a flatbed scanner at a resolution of 200 dpi and imported the socks image in TIFF file format into Adobe Photoshop. The feet image on the ribbon, also

PACKAGING PRESENTATION

scanned on a flatbed scanner at a resolution of 200 dpi, was taken from a collection of nineteenth-century engravings.

The three typefaces featured in this project include Madrone, Myriad, and Minion. The Madrone typeface was designed by Barbara Lind in 1991. Madrone was digitized from proofs of the wood type collection in the National Museum of American History in the Smithsonian Institution in Washington, D.C. A fat face roman, Madrone is typical of popular early nineteenth-century styles. Fat face types are characterized by their squatness and extreme letter width; one familiar version of this design is Bodoni Ultra Bold. Madrone is eye-catching for display uses in advertising and packaging.

Myriad is an Adobe Originals typeface designed by Carol Twombly and Robert Slimbach in 1992. Myriad, a multiple master typeface, is a sans serif design that allows the generation of thousands of individual fonts from one master typeface by interactively varying the design attributes of weight and width. Myriad makes a good text face as well as providing flexibility for filling display needs in all sizes and mediums.

Minion is a 1990 Adobe Originals typeface by Robert Slimbach. Minion is inspired by classical, old style typeface of the late Renaissance, a period of elegant, beautiful, and highly readable type designs. Created primarily for text setting, Minion

combines the aesthetic qualities that make text type highly readable with the versatility of digital technology. The Minion family contains a black weight, display, and swash fonts, expert sets, and a full range of ornaments, for uses that range from limited-edition books to newsletters to packaging.

To create the ribbon that wraps around the socks, you will use the pen tool to draw the two paths that outline the entire ribbon and diamond pattern. This project also covers:

• Selecting an image with the Color Range command

• Rotating a document

• Customizing the display of the transparent background using the Transparency command

• Drawing curved and straight-line paths with the pen tool

• Creating a clipping group

• Merging layers

• Inverting an image.

It should take you about 90 minutes s to complete this project.

Viewing the final image

1 Before launching the Adobe Photoshop application, throw away the Adobe Photoshop Preferences file to ensure all settings are returned to their default values.

2 Make sure the Madrone, Myriad, and Minion fonts from the *Advanced Adobe Photoshop* CD-ROM disc are installed.

3 Launch the Adobe Photoshop application, and open the *07Final.psd* file in *07Project* to view the final image.

The Layers palette contains the seven layers used to create this document.

4 Experiment with hiding and showing layers in the Layers palette to display the three color variations and the three fonts.

5 Position the *07Final.psd* document in the upper-right corner of your desktop to use it as a visual reference.

Opening an Adobe Photoshop document

For this example you will create a new document from an existing Adobe Photoshop document, allowing you to use its image and existing file specifications.

1 Open the *Socks.psd* file in *07Project*.

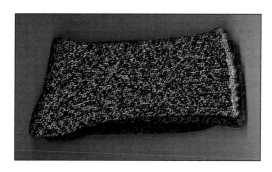

The socks image rests on a blue-colored background.

2 Save the *Socks.psd* file as *07Work.psd* to *Projects*.

PLACING THE SOCKS IMAGE

After opening and renaming an existing Adobe Photoshop document, you will use the Color Range command to select the socks image from the blue background and rotate the entire document using the Rotate command.

To airbrush a drop shadow behind the socks image, you will place the socks image on a layer with a transparent background that you can paint behind. This means you will duplicate the Background layer, rename the duplicated Background layer, and delete the white background color on the duplicated layer.

Using the Color Range command

After using the Color Range command to select the blue background, you will delete the blue background.

1 Choose Color Range from the Select menu, in the Color Range dialog box, make sure Sampled Colors from the Select pop-up menu is selected, the Fuzziness slider is set to 40, the Selection option is selected, and choose None from the Selection Preview pop-up menu.

2 Before closing the dialog box, click the blue background color in the document window of *07Work.psd* file, hold down the Shift key, and click any unselected portions of the blue background until the Preview window displays the background to be completely selected as shown in the illustration below.

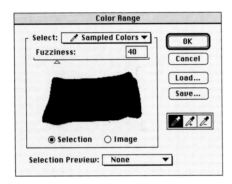

Note: The black portions over the socks image in the Preview window indicate areas not selected.

3 With the background completely selected (masked in white in the Preview window), click OK in the Color Range dialog box.

The document window displays a moving marquee, indicating the blue background is selected.

4 With the background color set to white, press the Delete key to delete the blue background.

The document window displays the socks image resting on the default white background.

5 Deselect the background.

Rotating the socks document

You will rotate the socks document to an upright position.

1 With everything deselected, choose Rotate from the Image menu and 90° CW (clockwise) from the submenu.

The entire document is rotated.

Airbrushing a drop shadow

After placing the socks image on a transparent layer, you will airbrush along the left and bottom edges of the socks with the airbrush tool set to Behind mode. Painting with the Behind mode has the effect similar to painting on the back of a piece of acetate. Only transparent areas are affected.

1 Double-click the airbrush tool, and in the Airbrush Options palette try to choose Behind from the Mode pop-up menu.

Behind mode is deactivated in the Mode pop-up menu since the Background layer has a default white background, impossible to paint behind.

To be able to paint behind the socks image, you must duplicate the Background layer to place the socks image on a layer with transparent background.

2 In the Layers palette choose Duplicate Layer from the Layers palette menu, in the Duplicate Layer dialog box type **Socks layer** to be the name of the duplicated layer, and click OK.

3 Hide the Background layer (eye icon not visible), and make sure the Socks layer is selected in the Layers palette.

The document window displays the socks image resting on a white background. Unlike the Background layer, it is possible to display transparent areas on the Socks layer.

4 Select the magic wand tool, click the white background in the document window, and press the Delete key.

The document window displays the socks image resting on a checkerboard background, indicating the transparent areas of the Socks layer.

5 Show the Background layer (eye icon visible), and make sure the Socks layer is selected in the Layers palette.

6 Deselect the selection.

7 Double-click the airbrush tool, in the Airbrush Options palette choose Behind from the Mode pop-up menu, and set the Pressure to 20%.

8 In the Brushes palette select the 100-pixel, soft-edged brush.

9 With the Socks layer selected in the Layers palette, airbrush along the left and bottom edges of the socks image to achieve the effect shown in the illustration below.

Note: To achieve a darker stroke, drag the paint more slowly or paint a second stroke over the first stroke.

10 Save the *07Work.psd* file.

Customizing the transparent layer display

By default, the transparent areas of a layer are displayed as a gray and white checkerboard pattern. The Transparency command gives you the ability to choose how you want to view the transparent areas.

1 Choose Preferences from the File menu and Transparency from the submenu, in the Transparency dialog box click the Large option from the Grid size box, choose Red from the Set pop-up menu, and click OK.

The document window displays the transparent background as a pink checkerboard.

2 In the Layers palette make sure the Socks layer and the Background layer are displayed (eye icons visible).

The document window displays the white background of the Background layer through the transparent areas of the Socks layer.

USING THE PEN TOOL

While you may be most familiar with using the pen tool to make smooth anti-aliased selections, for this project you will draw two paths: a curved path that outlines the ribbon and a straight-line path to outline the diamond pattern within the ribbon.

Drawing a curved path

A path is any line or shape you draw using the Adobe Photoshop pen tool in the Paths palette. The pen tool lets you draw smoothed-edged straight lines or smooth, flowing curves with precision. The pen tool in Adobe Photoshop works like the pen tool in Adobe Illustrator™.

Time out for a movie

If your system is capable of running Adobe Teach movies, you can see a preview of the technique used to draw the ribbon using the pen tool that is covered in this section. Play the movie named Pen Tool. For information on how to play Adobe Teach movies, see the "What You Need To Do" section at the beginning of this book.

1 Choose Show Rulers from the Window menu to display the rulers.

2 Drag the *07Final.psd* document window just to the right of the *07Work.psd* document window so that you have a visual reference when drawing the paths.

3 In the Layers palette click the New Layer icon, in the New Layer dialog box type **Ribbon layer** in the Name box, and click OK.

4 Make sure the Ribbon layer is selected in the Layers palette.

5 In the Paths palette select the pen tool (second tool from the left).

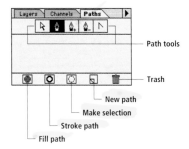

You create a path by clicking to set *anchor points*; you adjust the shape of the path by dragging the anchor points or the *direction lines* associated with each anchor point.

The ribbon will look more realistic if its edges are curved slightly outward, so use the pen tool to draw a curved path that includes the six anchor points.

6 Draw the path as shown in the following illustration, clicking the first anchor point to close the path.

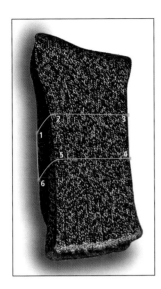

Note: To delete an anchor point, press the Delete key once. To erase the entire path, press the Delete key twice.

7 Select the arrow tool (the left-most tool in the Paths palette), and adjust the position of individual anchor points if necessary or adjust the direction lines of selected anchor points.

Note: Each time you click the corner tool on an anchor point, the point toggles between a smooth point and a corner point.

8 Double-click the Work Path in the Paths palette, in the Save Path dialog box type **Ribbon path** in the Name box, and click OK.

Colorizing the ribbon path

After using the Load Swatches command to replace the contents of the Swatches palette with a stored palette, you will colorize the Ribbon path. You will also lower the opacity of the fill to create the effect of a slightly transparent mylar-type ribbon.

1 In the Swatches palette choose Load Swatches from the Swatches palette menu, and when prompted choose *Swatches.aco* from the *07Project* file and click Open.

The Swatches palette displays six color swatches.

2 In the Swatches palette position the eyedropper over the left-most color swatch and click to set the foreground color to blue.

3 Make sure the Ribbon layer is selected in the Layers palette.

4 In the Paths palette choose Fill Path from the Paths palette menu, in the Fill Path dialog box type **90%** in the Opacity box, and click OK.

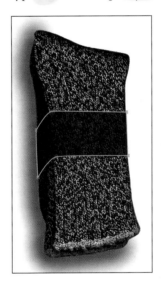

5 Save the *07Work.psd* file.

Drawing a straight-line path

You will draw a straight-line path that outlines the diamond pattern on the ribbon.

1 Make sure the Ribbon layer is selected in the Layers palette.

2 In the Paths palette click the New Path icon (second from the right in the bottom row), in the New Path dialog box type **Diamond path** in the Name box, and click OK.

3 With the pen tool selected in the Paths palette, click the first anchor point in the lower-left corner of the ribbon.

4 Continue drawing a six-anchor-point, zigzag-shaped path ending in the upper-right corner of the ribbon.

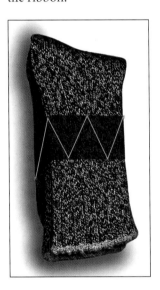

5 Move the cursor to the lower-right corner of the ribbon and click to create the seventh anchor point. From there, draw the last five anchor points as another zigzag shape.

6 Click the first anchor point to close the path.

7 To adjust the anchor points, select the arrow tool in the Paths palette (the left-most tool) and drag individual anchor points until they are evenly spaced.

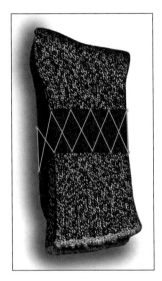

Colorizing the diamonds

You will colorize the diamond path with another color selected from the customized Swatches palette.

1 Make sure the Ribbon layer is selected in the Layers palette.

2 In the Swatches palette position the eyedropper over the second color swatch from the left and click to set the foreground color to cinnamon.

3 In the Paths palette choose Fill Subpath from the Paths palette menu, in the Fill Subpath dialog box type **90%** in the Opacity box, and click OK.

4 In the Paths palette click in the empty space below the paths to deselect all paths.

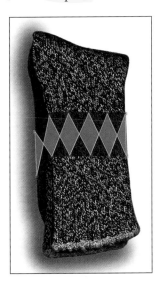

PLACING IMAGES AND TYPE

After placing the images and type to create a complete mock-up, you will create two more versions of the mock-up using different colors and fonts.

Placing the logo

After positioning an elliptical selection in the image, you will create a new layer from the floating selection.

1 With the Ribbon layer selected in the Layers palette, double-click the marquee tool, in the Marquee Options palette choose Elliptical from the Shape pop-up menu, choose Fixed Size from the Style pop-up menu, and type **160** pixels in the Width box and **72** pixels in the Height box.

2 Click anywhere on the ribbon and drag to center the ellipse on the diamonds.

3 Choose Float from the Select menu, and fill the selection with any color at 100% opacity.

4 In the Layers palette double-click the Floating Selection, in the Make Layer dialog box type **Logo layer** in the Name box, and click OK.

5 Save the *07Work.psd* file.

CREATING THE LOGO

After copying the feet image from the *Feet.psd* file to your working document, you will group two layers into a clipping group, allowing you to scale and position the feet image within the bounds of the elliptical logo.

Placing the feet image

You will drag a layer from the *Feet.psd* file to the *07Work.psd* file, adding the Feet layer to the *07Work.psd* file.

1 With the Logo layer selected in the Layers palette for the *07Work.psd* file, open the *Feet.psd* file in *07Project*.

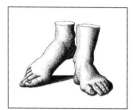

2 Drag the Feet layer from the Layers palette of the *Feet.psd* file to the document window of the *07Work.psd* file.

The Layers palette for the *07Work.psd* file displays the Feet layer, and the document window displays the feet image, considerably larger than the ellipse.

Creating a clipping group

You will group the Logo layer and the Feet layer into a clipping group, making it easier to position the feet image within the bounds of the elliptical logo.

Clipping groups enable you to define a selection on one layer as a mask for one or more layers above. For example, if you have a shape on one layer, a texture on the next layer, and some text on a third layer, you can define all three layers as a clipping group so that the texture and the text appear only through the shape. In a clipping group, the bottom layer in the group (called the base layer) controls the mode and transparency of all other layers in the group. Note that only successive layers can be included in a clipping group. If you ungroup a layer from a clipping group, it becomes the new base layer for any layers grouped above it.

1 In the Layers palette hold down the Option key (or Alt key), and position the cursor over the solid dividing line between the Logo layer and the Feet layer.

The cursor is displayed as the grouping cursor over the solid dividing line as shown in the illustration below.

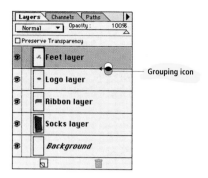

Grouping icon

2 In the Layers palette click the solid dividing line between the Logo layer and the Feet layer to group the two layers.

The Layers palette indicates a clipping group by dotted lines that separate the layers within the group. The name of the base layer, Logo layer, is underlined in the Layers palette.

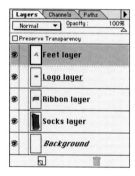

The document window displays the feet image clipping to the ellipse. Since the feet image is too large for the ellipse, you will scale and position the feet image.

3 With the Feet layer selected in the Layers palette and with the Info palette open, choose Effects from the Image menu and Scale from the submenu.

4 Hold down the Shift key (to maintain the current proportions), and drag the handles until the Info palette indicates a change of height and width of 53%, and confirm the scale.

5 With the Feet layer selected in the Layers palette and with the move tool selected, drag in the document window to position the feet to be centered within the ellipse.

With the feet image clipping to the ellipse, it is possible to get the best positioning since you can see the image as it applies to the shape.

Merging layers

Now that the feet image is scaled and positioned, you will merge the clipping group into a single layer, apply the Sharpen filter, and stroke the edge of the ellipse with black.

1 In the Layers palette make sure the Feet layer and the Logo layer are the only visible layers, make sure one of the layers to be merged is selected, and choose Merge Layers from the Layers palette menu.

Both layers are merged into the bottom-most layer, the Logo layer.

2 Sometimes an image may be slightly blurred after resizing, so choose Sharpen from the Filter menu and Sharpen from the submenu to focus the feet image and improve its clarity.

Stroking the logo image

After selecting the logo image using the Load Selection command, you will stroke the edge of the logo with black.

1 With the foreground color set to black and with the Logo layer selected in the Layers palette, choose Load Selection from the Select menu. In the Load Selection dialog box make sure Logo layer Transparency is selected in the Channel pop-up menu, and click OK.

The document window displays the logo image as selected.

2 Choose Stroke from the Edit menu, in the Stroke dialog box enter **4** pixels in the Width box, and click OK.

3 Make sure all layers are displayed, and close the *Feet.psd* file.

Inverting the feet image

After selecting the right half of the feet image, you will use the Invert command to create a negative of the feet image.

1 Double-click the marquee tool, and in the Marquee Options palette choose Rectangular from the Shape pop-up menu and Normal from the Style pop-up menu.

2 With the Logo layer selected in the Layers palette, drag a selection marquee over the right half portion of the ellipse, with the right edge of the marquee almost touching the right edge of the ellipse.

3 Choose Map from the Image menu and Invert from the submenu to create a negative of the selected image.

Only the interior of the ellipse is affected because all other portions are transparency protected.

4 Deselect the inverted image.

Placing the small box

After placing the small box in the center of the ellipse, you will colorize the box using colors selected from the customized Swatches palette.

1 Double-click the marquee tool, in the Marquee Options palette make sure Rectangular is selected in the Shape pop-up menu, choose Fixed Size from the Style pop-up menu, and type **32** pixels in the Width box and **24** pixels in the Height box.

2 With the Logo layer selected in the Layers palette, click the center of the label, hold down the mouse button and drag to center the box as shown in the illustration below.

Note: When positioning a selection marquee, hold down the Option key (or Alt key), and drag to center the marquee.

3 In the Swatches palette position the eyedropper over the left-most color swatch, and click to set the foreground color to deep blue.

4 Fill the box with the selected deep blue color.

5 In the Swatches palette position the eyedropper over the second color swatch from the left, and click to set the foreground color to cinnamon.

6 With the box still selected, choose Stroke from the Edit menu, in the Stroke dialog box select the Center option and type **2** pixels in the Width box, and click OK.

7 Deselect the box, and save the *07Work.psd* file.

PLACING THE G TYPE

You will place a large G in the small box on the Logo layer.

1 With the foreground color set to white, make sure the Logo layer is selected in the Layers palette.

2 Click the type tool, click the center of the box, in the Type Tool dialog box choose Madrone from the Font pop-up menu, type **15** points in the Size box, select the center alignment option, type an uppercase **G** in the text box, and click OK.

3 With the edges of the selection hidden, use the arrow keys to center the type in the box in one-pixel increments.

4 Deselect the type.

PLACING THE GÄNGSTIG TYPE

After placing the type on a layer of its own, you will duplicate the Type layer twice to create three Type layers, each layer displaying a different font.

Using the Madrone font

1 In the Layers palette click the New Layer icon in the lower-left corner, in the New Layer dialog box type **Type layer** in the Name box, and click OK.

2 Make sure the Type layer is selected in the Layers palette.

3 With the foreground color set to white, select the type tool, click in the document window just below the logo image, in the Type Tool dialog box choose Madrone from the Font pop-up menu, and type **15** points in the Size box.

4 Type "Gängstig" in the text box.

Macintosh platform: Type an uppercase **G,** *hold down the Option key, type* **u** *to specify the umlaut, type a lowercase* **a***, type* **ngstig** *in lowercase letters.*

Windows platform: Type an uppercase **G,** *hold down the Alt key as you type* **0228** *on the numeric keypad, type* **ngstig** *in lowercase letters.*

5 In the Type Tool dialog box drag to select the type in the text box, copy the selection to the Clipboard, and click OK.

6 With the move tool selected, drag to center the selected type under the logo.

7 Hold down the Option key (or Alt key) and drag away from the selected type to duplicate it.

8 With the duplicate type selected, choose Rotate from the Image menu and 180° from the submenu.

9 Drag to center the rotated, duplicate type above the logo.

10 Deselect the type.

Using the Myriad font

1 Hide the Type layer (eye icon not visible).

2 In the Layers palette click the New Layer icon, in the New Layer dialog box enter **Type 2 layer** in the Name box, and click OK.

3 With the Type 2 layer selected in the Layers palette, select the type tool, click in the document window just below the logo image, in the Type Tool dialog box choose Myriad Black from the Font pop-up menu, and type **18** points in the Size box and **10** in the Spacing box.

4 In the Type Tool dialog box paste the copied type from the Clipboard to the text box, and click OK

5 In the document window position, duplicate, and rotate the type as before.

6 Deselect the type.

Using the Minion font

1 Hide the Type 2 layer (eye icon not visible).

2 In the Layers palette click the New Layer icon in the lower-left corner, in the New Layer dialog box enter **Type 3 layer** in the Name box, and click OK.

3 With the Type 3 layer selected in the Layers palette, select the type tool, click in the document window just below the logo image, in the Type Tool dialog box choose Minion Black from the Font pop-up menu, and type **18** points in the Size box and **10** in the Spacing box.

4 In the Type Tool dialog box paste the copied type from the Clipboard to the text box, and click OK.

5 In the document window position, duplicate, and rotate the type as before.

6 Deselect the type.

7 Make sure the Type 2 layer and the Type 3 layer are positioned above the Type layer in the Layers palette.

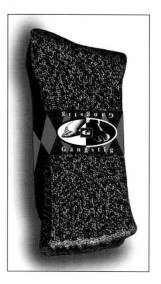

8 Save the *07Work.psd* file.

CREATING COLOR VARIATIONS OF THE RIBBON LAYER

After creating two more versions of the Ribbon layer, you will view various combinations of color and type.

1 In the Layers palette select and hide the Ribbon layer (eye icon not visible).

2 In the Layers palette click the New Layer icon in the lower-left corner, in the New Layer dialog box type **Ribbon 2 layer** in the Name box, type **90**% in the Opacity box, and click OK.

3 Make sure the Ribbon 2 layer is selected in the Layers palette.

4 In the Swatches palette select the green swatch (third from the left).

5 In the Paths palette select the Ribbon path, and click the Fill Path icon in the bottom-left corner.

6 In the Swatches palette select the blue swatch (fourth from the left).

7 In the Paths palette select the Diamond path, and click the Fill Path icon in the bottom-left corner.

8 Hide the Ribbon 2 layer (eye icon not visible).

9 In the Layers palette click the New Layer icon, in the New Layer dialog box type **Ribbon 3 layer** in the Name box, type **90**% in the Opacity box, and click OK.

10 Make sure the Ribbon 3 layer is selected in the Layers palette.

11 In the Swatches palette select the maroon swatch (fifth from the left).

12 In the Paths palette select the Ribbon path, and click the Fill Path icon in the bottom-left corner.

13 In the Swatches palette select the right-most swatch to set the foreground color to lilac.

14 In the Paths palette select the Diamond path, and click the Fill Path icon in the bottom-left corner of the palette.

15 In the Layers palette make sure the Ribbon 2 layer and the Ribbon 3 layer are positioned above the Ribbon layer.

16 In the Layers palette show and hide various type and color combinations.

17 Save the *07Work.psd* file, close all open files, and quit (or exit) the Adobe Photoshop application.

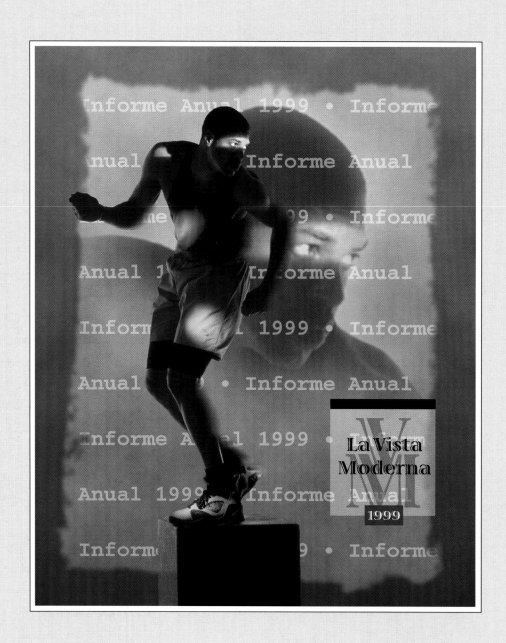

La Vista
Moderna

VM

1999

• B R A Z I L •

8

You will create the front cover for the 1999 Annual Report for La Vista Moderna, a Brazialian company producing state-of-the-art fitness-

ANNUAL REPORT COVER

wear. The athlete, photographed on a white background, has spotlights trained on sections of his face and body. ■ This project places emphasis on how to **manage the size of your file** as you work. The approach featured in this project includes **merging layers more frequently to** reduce your file size. To incorporate another file management technique, you will use the Apply Image command to apply an image from one file to another file without adding a new layer to the target file.

The font used for the La Vista Moderna logo is taken from the Viva MM typeface family. Viva, designed by Carol Twombly, was released in 1993 as the first open-face design in the Adobe Originals Library. Viva is a multiple master typeface with the

ANNUAL REPORT COVER

weight and width axis that allow variations of Viva to be generated by the user. Viva font's weight axis can be thought of as a shadow axis: as the weight increases, the design casts a longer shadow in a weight range from light to bold. Viva font's width axis ranges from condensed to extra-extended. The display possibilities are essentially unlimited; the generated variations allow for legible copyfitting in advertising, book titles, posters, and any display material that needs an original look.

This project covers:

• Using the gradient tool

• Applying the Cloud filter to an alpha channel

• Applying the Motion Blur filter

• Adjusting the levels of a grayscale image

• Creating a mask from a charcoal sketch

• Using the Apply Image command.

It should take you about 2 hours to complete this project.

Viewing the final image

1 Before launching the Adobe Photoshop application, throw away the Adobe Photoshop Preferences file to ensure all settings are returned to their default values.

2 Make sure the Viva font is installed.

3 Launch the Adobe Photoshop application, and open the *08Final.psd* file in *08Project* to view the final image.

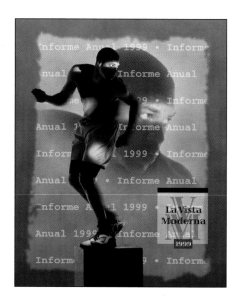

4 Reduce the view of the *08Final.psd* document, and position it in the upper-right corner of your desktop for use as a visual reference.

Opening a new document

1 Create a new document, in the New dialog box, type **08Work.psd** to name the file, and enter **572** pixels in the Width box, **700** pixels in the Height box, and **100** pixels per inch in the Resolution box, and click OK.

By default the document window displays the default white background, and the Layers palette displays the Background layer.

CREATING A BACKGROUND IMAGE

After applying a gradient fill to the Background layer, you will apply the Difference Clouds filter to an alpha channel, load the selection, and then adjust the brightness and contrast of the selection to create a mottled effect in the background image.

Next, you will use the lasso tool to select the head and shoulders of the athlete image stored in another file, and then drag the selected image to your working document.

TIP: TO CREATE A NEW CHANNEL, CLICK THE NEW CHANNEL ICON, THE MIDDLE ICON AT THE BOTTOM OF THE CHANNELS PALETTE.

Applying a gradient fill

You will use the gradient tool to fill the Background layer with a gradual transition from a deep brown to a light brown.

1 To set the foreground color to deep brown, set the RGB sliders in the Picker palette to the following values:

    Red 85
    Green 44
    Blue 12

2 To set the background color to light brown, set the RGB sliders in the Picker palette to the following values:

    Red 202
    Green 138
    Blue 87

3 With the Background layer selected in the Layers palette and with the gradient tool selected, hold down the Shift key (to constrain the angle to 90°), drag straight up from the bottom-center edge of the document to the top-center edge, and release the mouse button.

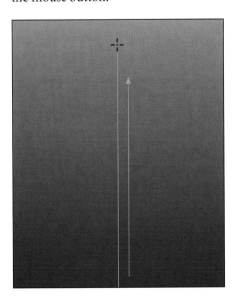

4 Save the *08Work.psd* file to *Projects*.

Applying the Difference Clouds filter to an alpha channel

After placing a cloud image into a newly created alpha channel, you will load the channel and adjust the Brightness and Contrast of the cloud image to create a mottled effect for the background.

1 In the Channels palette choose New Channel from the Channels palette menu, in the Channel Options dialog box type **Clouds mask channel** in the Name box, and click OK.

2 With the Clouds mask channel selected in the Channels palette for the *08Work.psd* file, choose Render from the Filter menu and Difference Clouds from the submenu to place a clouds image into the Clouds mask channel.

3 In the Channels palette select the RGB channel.

4 Choose Load Selection from the Select menu, in the Load Selection dialog box make sure *08Work.psd* is selected from the Document pop-up menu and make sure Clouds mask channel is selected from the Channel pop-up menu, and click OK.

The document window displays the portions of the clouds that are selected.

Note: You may get a slightly different selection from the one illustrated below.

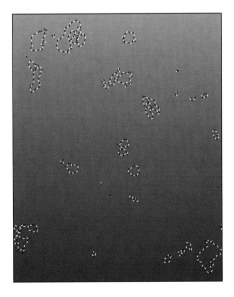

TIP: TO LOAD A CHAN-
NEL AS A SELECTION,
MAKE SURE THE TARGET
CHANNEL IS SELECTED,
HOLD DOWN THE OP-
TION KEY (OR ALT KEY),
AND CLICK THE SOURCE
CHANNEL. OR, WITH
THE TARGET CHANNEL
SELECTED, DRAG THE
SOURCE CHANNEL TO
THE LOAD SELECTION
ICON IN THE LOWER-
LEFT CORNER OF THE
CHANNELS PALETTE.

You will adjust the brightness and contrast of the selected areas.

5 Hide the edges of the selection.

6 Choose Adjust from the Image menu and then choose Brightness/Contrast from the submenu, in the Brightness/Contrast dialog box enter **60** in the Brightness box and **70** in the Contrast box, and click OK.

The background has a mottled effect.

Note: Even though the Brightness/Contrast command makes very generalized adjustments to the tonal range of an image, in this example it works fine for our creative purposes.

7 Save the *08Work.psd* file.

Placing the background athlete image

After selecting a portion of the athlete image in the *Athlete.psd* file and dragging the selection to the *08Work.psd* file, you will create a new layer and adjust its opacity.

1 Open the *Athlete.psd* file in *08Project*, make sure the Athlete layer is selected, and zoom in once on the head and upper torso of the image.

2 Double-click the lasso tool, and in the Lasso Options palette, enter **15** pixels in the Feather box.

3 Drag the lasso tool just along the outside of the head and shoulders.

Note: In this example, making a rough selection of the athlete with the 15-pixel feather produces a desired white ghosting effect.

4 With the move tool selected, drag the selection from the document window of the *Athlete.psd* file to the document window of the *08Work.psd* file, and drag to position the selection in the very upper-right corner.

The Layers palette displays a Floating Selection.

5 With the Info palette open, choose Effects from the Image menu and Scale from the submenu.

TIP: IN THE LAYERS PALETTE DOUBLE-CLICK A FLOATING SELECTION TO MAKE IT A LAYER.

6 Hold down the Shift key (to maintain a proportional scale), and drag the lower-left handle down and left (past the edges of the work canvas if necessary) until the Info palette shows the percentage change in width and height equal to about 375%.

7 Click the gavel icon inside the selection to confirm the scale.

Note: Click outside of the selection to undo the scale.

8 With the move tool selected, drag in the document window to position the athlete image.

9 In the Layers palette drag the Floating Selection to the New Layer icon, in Make Layer dialog box type **Background athlete layer** in the Name box and enter **65**% in the Opacity box, and click OK.

10 Save the *08Work.psd* file.

MERGING LAYERS

Now that the layer contents for the Background layer and the Background athlete layer are finalized, you will merge the two layers into a single layer, the Background layer, and then apply the repeating type to the background image.

1 With the Background athlete layer and the Background layer displayed (eye icons visible), choose Merge Layers from the Layers palette menu in the Layers palette.

Note: One of the layers to be merged must be selected in the Layers palette to activate the Merge Layers command.

CREATING A BORDER SELECTION

After adjusting the Levels of a charcoal image, you will apply the Gaussian Blur filter and adjust the brightness and contrast, ultimately creating a mask that you will load to select the border of the document.

Adjusting the levels of the charcoal image

This charcoal sketch was scanned on a 24-bit flatbed scanner at a resolution of 200 dpi.

1 Open the *Charcoal.psd* file in *08Project*.

TIP: TO FILL A SELEC-
TION WITH THE FORE-
GROUND COLOR,
HOLD DOWN THE
OPTION KEY (OR ALT
KEY) AND PRESS THE
DELETE KEY.

2 Choose Adjust from the Image menu and Levels from the submenu, and take a moment to view the histogram for the charcoal image in the Levels dialog box.

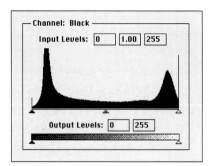

A histogram plots the brightness values versus the number of pixels at each level. The darkest pixels appear at the left; the brightest pixels appear at the right. The histogram indicates that the image has an abundance of high tones (whites) and low tones (blacks) with some midtones as well.

Looking closely at the image, you can see the light gray tones throughout it. To create a mask from this image, it will be necessary to adjust the levels of this image so that the midtones are eliminated, allowing the rough-edged sketch to be masked.

Even though the Threshold command converts grayscale or color images to high-contrast black-and-white images, the Levels command not only allows for more precise adjustments, but the overall effect worked better for our purposes.

3 In the Levels dialog box drag the left-most and right-most triangles below the histogram toward the center of the slider until the Input Levels are set to **121**, **1.00**, and **175,** and click OK.

Note: The black triangle controls the shadows, the gray triangle controls the midtones or gamma, and the white triangle controls the highlights.

4 To view the new histogram for the charcoal sketch, choose Adjust from the Image menu and Histogram from the submenu.

The histogram shows that changing the Input Levels has increased the contrast of the image.

5 Click OK to close the histogram.

6 With the magic wand selected, choose All from the Select menu, hold down the Command key (or Ctrl key) to subtract from a selection, and click the white background.

The black image is selected.

7 Fill the selection with black.

8 Deselect the image, and save the *08Work.psd* file.

Editing the edge of the charcoal image

We found that blurring and then adjusting the brightness and contrast of the charcoal image gave the best results.

The Gaussian Blur filter quickly blurs an image by an adjustable amount. This filter adds low-frequency detail, and can produce a hazy effect.

1 Choose Blur from the Filter menu and Gaussian Blur from the submenu, in the Gaussian Blur dialog box enter **10** pixels in the Radius box, and click OK.

You will adjust the brightness and contrast of the charcoal image to sharpen its edge.

2 Choose Adjust from the Image menu and Brightness/Contrast from the submenu, in the Brightness/Contrast dialog box enter **0** in the Brightness box and **55** in the Contrast box, and click OK.

Creating an alpha channel

You will drag the channel from the Channels palette of the *Charcoal.psd* file to the document window of the *08Work.psd* file to copy the border mask (or selection) from one file to another file.

1 With the *08Work.psd* file active and with the *Charcoal.psd* file active, drag the Black channel from the Channels palette of the *Charcoal.psd* file to the document window of the *08Work.psd* file.

The Channels palette for the *08Work.psd* document displays alpha channel #5.

2 Double-click alpha channel #5, in the Channel Options dialog box type **Border mask** in the Name box, and click OK.

3 Close the *Charcoal.psd* file without saving changes, deselect everything in the *08Work.psd* file, and save the *08Work.psd* file.

USING THE APPLY IMAGE COMMAND

You will use the Apply Image command to apply the repeating Informe Anual 1999 type to the Background layer in the *08Work.psd* file. "Informe Anual" is Spanish for Annual Report.

The Apply Image command works by manipulating the corresponding pixels in a source layer and target layer (in a single file or in two files, provided both files have the same dimensions and resolution) and placing the resulting pixels in a single target layer.

Note: If extra disk space is in short supply, it is useful to use the Apply Image command because it allows you to apply one layer to another without adding a layer or floating selection.

1 Open the *Type.psd* file in *08Project*.

```
Informe Anual 1999 • Informe

Anual 1999 • Informe Anual

Informe Anual 1999 • Informe

Anual 1999 • Informe Anual

Informe Anual 1999 • Informe

Anual 1999 • Informe Anual

Informe Anual 1999 • Informe

Anual 1999 • Informe Anual

Informe Anual 1999 • Informe
```

The document window displays black type on a transparent background. In keeping with a traditional, business-world theme for our Annual Report cover, we created the type using the Courier Bold font.

2 With the Background layer selected in the Layers palette for the *08Work.psd* file, make sure everything is deselected, and choose Apply Image from the Image menu.

The Apply Image dialog box displays the currently active file, *08Work.psd,* as the target file and the Background layer as the target layer.

3 In the Apply Image dialog box click the Preview option, choose Type.psd from the Source pop-up menu, choose Type layer from the Layer pop-up menu, choose RGB from the Channel pop-up menu, and click the Invert option (to invert the black type to white).

4 In the Apply Image dialog box choose Lighter from the Blending pop-up menu, and enter **50%** in the Opacity box.

The Lighter option compares the brightness values of the corresponding pixels in the two layers and displays the lighter of the two.

5 In the Apply Image dialog box click the Mask option, make sure the *08Work.psd* file is selected from the pop-up menu, choose Background from the Layer pop-up menu, choose Border mask from the Channel pop-up menu, and click the Invert option (to invert the mask, selecting the interior of the Border mask).

The document window displays a preview of the current settings of the Apply Image dialog box, with edges of the type image masked by the Border mask channel.

6 Before you click OK, experiment with viewing the results of selecting different settings in the Apply Image dialog box, returning to the original settings when you have seen enough, and click OK.

The document window displays the type applied to the Background layer.

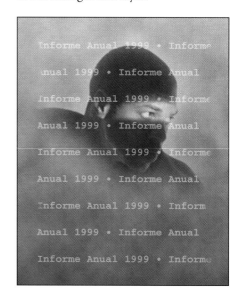

7 Close the *Type.psd* file.

USING QUICK MASK MODE

After selecting the white background of the athlete image with the magic wand tool, you will refine the selection using the Quick Mask mode. Quick Mask mode is used for creating and editing temporary masks in the document window.

Time out for a movie

If your system is capable of running Adobe Teach movies, you can see a preview of the technique used to refine the selection of the athlete image in Quick Mask mode that is covered in this section. Play the movie named Quick Mask. For information on how to play Adobe Teach movies, see the "What You Need To Do" section at the beginning of this book.

Selecting the athlete image

1 With the *Athlete.psd* file active, click the default colors icon.

2 Double-click the magic wand tool, and in the Magic Wand Options palette make sure the tolerance is set to 32.

3 Click the white background in the document window of the *Athlete.psd* file, hold down the Shift key, and click the gap between the torso and the arm so that the entire white background is selected.

The document window displays a marquee selection that indicates the right heel is included in the selected white background.

4 Magnify the view of the right heel, so that you can view how the part of the heel is selected.

5 Click the Quick Mask mode icon (one up from the lower-right corner) in the toolbox.

A red overlay covers all of the image except the selected area (the unprotected area). By default, Quick Mask mode colors the protected area using a red, 50% opaque overlay.

For the purpose of excluding parts of the athlete image that were included in the selection (not overlaid in red), you will add to the red overlay so that the athlete image is completely unselected (or overlaid in red).

6 Click the paintbrush tool, in the Brushes palette choose New Brush from the Brushes palette menu, in the New Brush dialog box type **4** pixels in the Diameter box, type **100**% in the Hardness box, and make sure Spacing is set to 25%, and click OK.

7 In the document window paint the selected portions of the heel (not overlaid in red) to completely mask (or unselect) the entire athlete image.

Note: Paint with white to erase the Quick mask.

8 Click the Standard mode icon (one up from the lower-left corner of the toolbox) to return to your original image.

The document window displays the selected white background.

PLACING THE ATHLETE IMAGE

After dragging the athlete image from the *Athlete.psd* file to the *08Work.psd* file, you will position it, remove the white matte from the edges of the image, and apply the Motion Blur filter.

1 Choose Inverse from the Select menu to select the athlete image, and drag the selection from the document window of the *Athlete.psd* file to the document window of the *08Work.psd* file.

2 With the *08Work.psd* file active and with the move tool selected, drag to position the athlete image in the work canvas just to the left of center, with the bottom of the pedestal about ½ inch below the bottom edge of the document window.

3 With the selection hidden, magnify the view of the elbow on the right until the white edge along the arm is displayed.

Since the athlete image was created on a white background, it is necessary to use the Remove White Matte command to eliminate the remnants of white around the edges of the image.

4 Choose Matting from the Select menu and Remove White Matte from the submenu.

5 In the Layers palette drag the Floating Selection to the New Layer icon in the lower-left corner, in the Make Layer dialog box type **Athlete layer** in the Name box, and click OK.

Applying the Motion Blur filter

The Motion Blur filter produces a blur effect in a particular direction and of a specific intensity. The effect of this filter is analogous to taking a picture of a moving object with a fixed exposure time.

1 Double-click the lasso tool, and in the Lasso Options palette enter **3** pixels in the Feather box.

2 Drag to select the arms, torso, and legs.

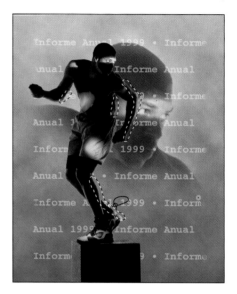

3 Choose Blur from the Filter menu and Motion Blur from the submenu, in the Motion Blur dialog box deselect the Preview option, position the cursor over the Preview window, drag to view a portion of the figure to be blurred, enter **4°** in the Angle box and **17** pixels in the Distance box, and click OK.

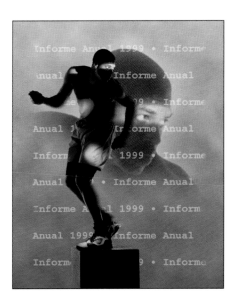

4 Close the *Athlete.psd* file, and save the *08Work.psd* file.

CREATING THE COLORIZED BORDER

To create the tortoise shell border, you will merge the layers, load the selection saved in an existing alpha channel, and then colorize the border by loading a stored color correction setting.

Merging layers

Before colorizing the border, you will merge the two existing layers into the Background layer.

1 With the Athlete layer and the Background layer displayed (eye icons visible), choose Merge Layers from the Layers palette menu in the Layers palette.

Both layers are merged into the Background layer.

Colorizing the border

After loading the selection saved in the Border mask channel, you will use the Hue/Saturation dialog box to load and apply a stored color correction setting to the selected border.

1 In the Channels palette for the *08Work.psd* file select the RGB channel, and drag the Border mask channel to the Load Selection icon in the lower-left corner of the Channels palette.

The document window displays the selected border.

2 With the Background layer selected in the Layers palette and with the edges of the selection hidden, choose Adjust from the Image menu and Hue/Saturation from the submenu, and in the Hue/Saturation dialog box click the Load button.

3 When prompted, make sure *08Set.hss* is selected from *08Project*, and click the Open button.

TIP: TO MOVE A SELEC-
TION IN ONE-PIXEL
INCREMENTS, PRESS
THE ARROW KEYS.

4 In the Hue/Saturation dialog box click OK to apply the stored color correction setting.

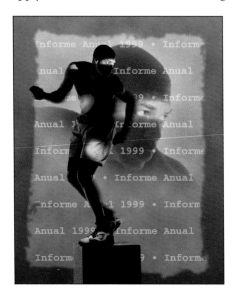

PLACING THE LOGO AND THE TYPE

After placing the logo box and the large-sized type on a new layer, you will place the name of the company and the 1999 type on another layer.

Creating the logo box

After placing the logo box on its own layer, you will use the Levels command to make the logo box image appear lighter.

1 Double-click the marquee tool, in the Marquee Options palette choose Rectangular from the Shape pop-up menu, choose Fixed Size from the Style pop-up menu, and enter **137** pixels in the Width box and **146** pixels in the Height box.

2 Click the document window, hold down the mouse button, and drag to position the rectangle so that its lower edge is aligned with the top of the pedestal and its right edge is about ½ inch from the right side of the document window as shown in the illustration below.

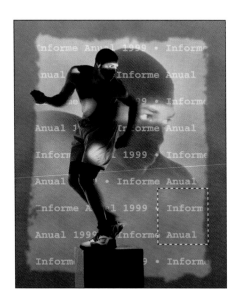

3 Float the selection.

4 In the Layers palette choose Make Layer from the Layers palette menu, in the Make Layer dialog box type **Logo layer** in the Name box, and click OK.

You will adjust the Output Levels slider controls at the bottom of the Levels dialog box to reduce the contrast in the logo. The black triangle controls the shadows, and the white triangle controls the highlights.

5 To make the logo box appear lighter, choose Adjust from the Image menu and Levels from the submenu, and position the Levels dialog box so that you can view the selection, click the Preview option to activate it, drag the left-most black triangle on the Output Levels slider to the right to setting 115, and click OK.

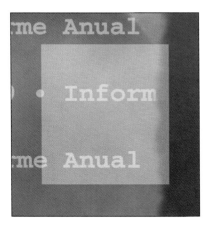

Narrowing the Output Level range reduces contrast in the image, reducing the darker levels in the logo box image.

6 Save the *08Work.psd* file.

Creating the black bar

You will create the black bar that runs across the top of the logo box.

1 Zoom in twice on the logo box.

2 Double-click the marquee tool, in the Marquee Options palette make sure Rectangular is selected from the Shape pop-up menu, Fixed Size is selected from the Style pop-up menu, and Width is set to 137 pixels, and enter **13** pixels in the Height box.

3 With Logo layer selected in the Layers palette, click the document window, hold down the mouse button, and drag to position the top edge of the selection to be aligned with the top edge of the logo box.

4 Fill the selection with black.

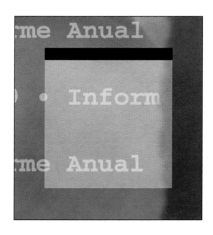

Placing the large type

You will place the "V" and the "M" that appear in the logo box.

1 Make sure the Logo layer is selected in the Layers palette.

2 Click the type tool, click the logo box in the document window, in the Type Tool dialog box choose Viva 700 MM 600 Norm from the Font pop-up menu, enter **70** points in the Size box, type an uppercase **V** in the text box, and click OK.

3 With the edges of the selected type hidden, drag to center the selected type in the upper portion of the logo box, about ⅛ inch below the black bar.

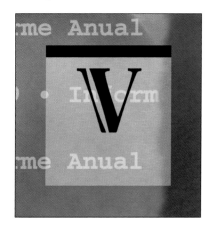

4 In the Layers palette set the Opacity slider to 30%.

5 Select the type tool, click the logo box in the document window, in the Type Tool dialog box type an uppercase **M** in the text box, and click OK to accept the previous settings.

6 With the edges of the selected type hidden, drag to center the selected type in the lower portion of the logo box, about ⅛ inch above the bottom edge of the logo box.

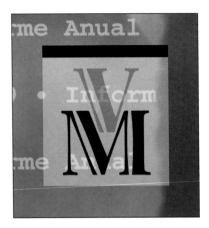

7 In the Layers palette set the Opacity slider to 30%.

8 Deselect the type, and save the *08Work.psd* file.

Placing the La Vista Moderna type

Before placing the La Vista Moderna type in the logo box, you will add a new layer for the type. To maintain design flexibility for the logo and the type, you will allow the Logo layer and the Type layer to remain intact.

1 In the Layers palette click the New Layer icon, in the New Layer dialog box type **Type layer** in the Name box, and click OK.

2 Select the type tool, click the logo box, in the Type Tool dialog box choose Viva 700 MM 600 Norm from the Font pop-up menu, enter **17** points in the Size box, and enter **21** in the Leading box, click the Center Alignment option, in the text box type **La Vista**, press the Return key (or the Enter key), type **Moderna**, and click OK.

3 With the edges of the selected type hidden, drag to position the type in the center of the logo box.

4 Deselect the type, and save the *08Work.psd* file.

Creating the 1999 box

The color of the box that contains '1999' is sampled from the tortoise shell border on the Background layer.

1 In the Layers palette select the Background layer.

2 Double-click the marquee tool, and with Rectangular selected in the Shape pop-up menu and Fixed Size selected in the Style pop-up menu, enter **50** pixels in the Width box and **25** pixels in the Height box.

3 Position the selection over the tortoise shell border, hold down the Option key (or Alt key), and drag to create a duplicate.

The Layers palette displays the duplicated image as a Floating Selection above the Background layer.

4 In the Layers palette drag the Floating Selection above the Type layer.

The Layers palette displays the Floating Selection above the Type layer.

5 In the document window drag to center the selected tortoise shell box on the lower edge of the white logo box.

Placing the 1999 type

1 Make sure the Type layer is selected in the Layers palette, and set the foreground color to white.

2 Select the type tool, click inside the red box, in the Type Tool dialog box make sure Viva 600 MM 700 Norm is selected in the Font pop-up menu, enter **12** points in the Size box, make sure the Center Alignment option is selected, type **1999** in the text box, and click OK.

3 Use the arrow keys to center the type in the red box.

4 Deselect the type, and save the *08Work.psd* file.

5 Double-click the hand tool to display the entire work canvas.

6 Save the *08Work.psd* file, close all open files, and quit (or exit) the Adobe Photoshop application.

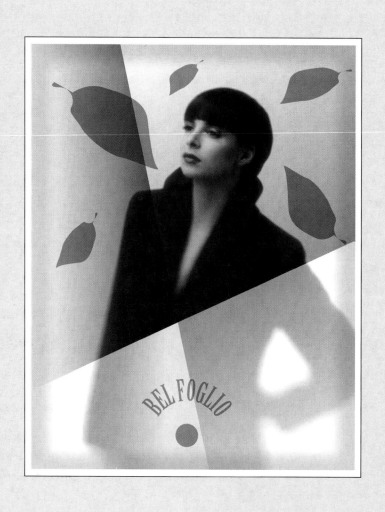

BEL FOGLIO

9

In this project you will create a newspaper advertisement for Italian clothing manufacturer Bel Foglio (meaning beautiful leaf). With a single black and white photograph as the central image, this project fea-

ADVERTISEMENT

tures using the new layer mask feature and using Adobe Illustrator to create type on a curved path. To edit the layer mask, you will select various portions of the layer mask and then apply the gradient tool, creating the four quadrants. ▪ Birch, the typeface used for the Bel Foglio logo, is an Adobe Originals typeface designed in 1990 by Adobe Designer Kim Buker. Birch is modeled after a Latin Condensed wood type found in an 1879 William Page specimen book. A particularly legible condensed display typeface, Birch is notable for its angled serifs.

To create type on a curved path, you will export a copy of your Adobe Photoshop working file into the Adobe Illustrator application. After scaling and positioning the type and some leaf-shaped line art in Adobe Illustrator, you will import the type and

ADVERTISEMENT LAYOUT

line art into the Adobe Photoshop application, placing them on a layer of their own. Lastly, this project shows you just how easy it is to convert this grayscale image into a duotone image, specifying two different inks to be used for printing.

The central image was scanned from a conventional single-color transparency at a resolution of 300 dpi. For the sake of reducing the demand for disk space on your system, you will execute the steps in this project with a file resolution of 100 ppi.

Some of the techniques covered in this project include:

• Adding a layer mask

• Exporting an Adobe Photoshop file to the Adobe Illustrator application

• Placing line art and type on a curved path in the Adobe Illustrator application

• Importing a file into Adobe Photoshop

• Adjusting the levels of a selection

• Adjusting the work canvas size

• Converting from grayscale mode to duotone mode.

It should take you about 90 minutes to complete this project.

Viewing the final image

Before beginning this project, open and view the final image.

1 Before launching the Adobe Photoshop application, throw away the Adobe Photoshop Preferences file to make sure all settings are returned to their default values.

2 Make sure the Birch font, found on the *Advanced Adobe Photoshop* CD-ROM disc, is installed.

3 Launch the Adobe Photoshop application, and open the *09Final.psd* file in *09Project* to view the final image.

4 Reduce the view of the *09Final.psd* document, and drag it to the upper-right corner of your desktop to use as a visual reference.

Opening an Adobe Photoshop file

Rather than creating a new file, you will open the existing Adobe Photoshop document, *Model.psd*.

1 Open the *Model.psd* file in *09Project*.

This black and white image was scanned from a 2¼ inch transparency at 300 dpi on a Leafscan 45 transparency scanner.

2 Save the file as *09Work.psd* to *Projects*.

ADDING A LAYER MASK

After adding a new layer and filling it with black, the model image is completely obscured. For this reason, you will add and edit a layer mask that will mask portions of the black-filled layer, making those portions transparent and allowing the model image to be visible.

Adding the Gradients layer

You will fill an entire layer with black, causing the model image to be hidden behind the Gradients layer.

1 In the Layers palette click the New Layer icon, in the New Layer dialog box type **Gradients layer** in the Name box, and click OK.

2 With Gradients layer selected in the Layers palette, fill the layer with black.

Note: Hold down the Option key (or Alt key) and press the Delete key to fill a selection with the foreground color.

The document window displays the Gradients layer filled with black.

Editing a layer mask

After adding a layer mask and selecting the left portion of the work canvas with the lasso tool, you will use the gradient tool to edit the layer mask so that portions of the black Gradients layer are masked (made transparent) by the layer mask, allowing you to view the model image through the Gradients layer.

1 With the Gradients layer selected in the Layers palette, choose Add Layer Mask from the Layers palette menu.

2 Double-click the lasso tool, and in the Lasso Options palette make sure the Feather is set to 0 pixels.

Note: To display the rulers, choose Show Rulers from the Window menu.

3 Make sure the mask thumbnail (right thumbnail) is selected to be the target in the Gradients layer in the Layers palette, and make sure the entire work canvas is displayed in the document window.

4 Hold down the Option key (or Alt key), click the upper-left corner of the work canvas, click the top edge about 4 inches from the left edge, click the bottom edge about 8 inches from the left edge, click the lower-left corner, and then click the upper-left corner, closing the selection as shown in the illustration below.

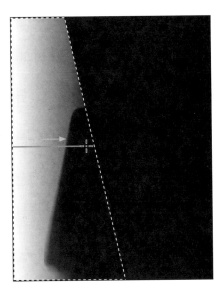

You will apply a gradient effect to the right portion of the work canvas.

6 Inverse the selection to select the right portion of the work canvas.

7 With the gradient tool selected, drag from the upper-left corner of the selection to the lower-right corner of the selection.

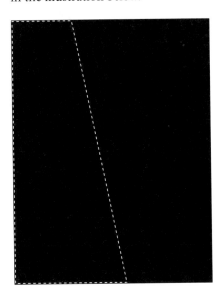

5 With the gradient tool selected and with the default colors selected, drag straight across from the center-left edge of the selection to the right edge of the selection.

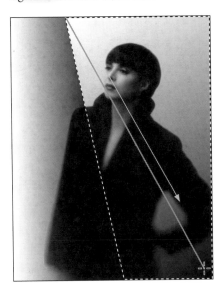

8 Deselect everything.

Inverting a selection

After using the lasso tool to select the bottom portion of the work canvas, you will invert the selection.

1 Select the lasso tool, and make sure the layer thumbnail (left thumbnail) is selected in the Gradients layer in the Layers palette.

2 Hold down the Option key (or Alt key), click the lower-left corner of the document, click the left edge about 3½ inches above the bottom edge, click the right edge about 10 inches above the bottom edge, click the lower-right corner, and click the lower-left corner, closing the selection.

3 With the layer thumbnail selected in the Gradients layer in the Layers palette, choose Map from the Image menu and Invert from the submenu to invert the selection from gray to white.

4 Deselect the bottom portion.

5 In the Layers palette choose Remove Layer mask from the Layers palette menu, and when prompted, click Apply to apply the layer mask to the Gradients layer.

6 In the Layers palette set the opacity for the Gradients layer to 85%.

7 Save the *09Work.psd* file.

USING ADOBE ILLUSTRATOR

As was mentioned before, to create type on a curved path, you will export a copy of your Adobe Photoshop working file into Adobe Illustrator. Adobe Illustrator is a leading illustration and page-design tool that allows you to create, manipulate, and refine artwork flexibly and accurately.

After scaling and positioning the type and some leaf-shaped line art in Adobe Illustrator, you will import the type and line art into Adobe Photoshop, placing them on a layer of their own.

Exporting a file to Adobe Illustrator

Exporting an Adobe Photoshop EPS file to Illustrator makes it possible to place the type on a curved path, and simplifies any sizing and placement of Adobe Illustrator artwork.

Note: If you do not have Adobe Illustrator installed, you can skip ahead to the section, PLACING THE LINE ART.

1 Choose Save a Copy from the File menu, and when prompted, make sure *Projects* is selected in the pop-up menu, type **09Work.eps** in the Name box, choose EPS from the Format pop-up menu, and click Save (or OK).

2 In the EPS dialog box click OK to accept all defaults, and close the Adobe Photoshop application.

Note: With enough memory, it is possible for the Adobe Photoshop program and the Adobe Illustrator program to be open at the same time.

The *09Work.eps* file is automatically flattened. Your current work file, *09Work.psd*, remains intact.

Placing artwork in Adobe Illustrator

1 Launch the Adobe Illustrator application, and open the Adobe Illustrator file, *Template.ai* in *09Project*.

Template.ai opens as an empty window with leaf-shaped line art that was drawn using the pen tool in Adobe Illustrator.

2 Choose Place Art from the File menu, and when prompted, select the *09Work.eps* file, and click Place.

3 Center the *09Work.eps* image in the *Template.ai* window.

4 Choose Send to Back from the Arrange menu to make the image the backmost object on its level.

5 Choose Lock from the Arrange menu to prevent the image from being moved or modified.

6 Choose Preview from the View menu.

7 Drag to arrange the leaves around the model.

Placing type on a curved path

Adobe Illustrator makes it possible to place the Bel Foglio type on a curved path.

1 Double-click the oval tool, click on the pasteboard, in the Oval dialog box type **3** in the Width box and **3** in the Height box, and click OK.

2 With the selection tool, drag to center the circle about one-half inch above the bottom edge of the place image.

3 Select the path type tool from the Type Tool pop-up menu in the toolbox.

4 Choose Character from the Type menu, in the Character palette choose Birch from the Font pop-up menu, choose 90 points from the Size pop-up menu, press Return to apply the selected font, and close the character.

5 Choose Paragraph from the Type menu, in the Paragraph palette make sure Center alignment is selected, press the Return key (or the Enter key), and close the paragraph.

6 Click the top-center edge of the type path, and type **BEL FOGLIO** in uppercase letters.

7 With the oval tool selected, click the center of the circle, in the Oval dialog box enter **1** inch in the Width box and **1** inch in the Height box, and click OK.

8 Drag to center the circle under the type.

PLACING THE LINE ART

After importing the line art into Adobe Illustrator as paths, you will adjust its positioning of the paths, fill the paths with black, and adjust the opacity of the line art image.

Note: If you skipped the Adobe Illustrator portion of this project, copy and paste the Paths *file in* 09Project *to a new layer in the* 09Work.psd *file, and resume executing at Step 8 of this section.*

Importing a file into Adobe Photoshop

Before you import the file into Adobe Photoshop, you will delete the black and white image, so that only the line art (leaves and logo) is exported.

1 With the selection tool, click the baseline of the type path to select it.

2 If necessary, you may use the move tool to center the type.

3 Choose Create Outlines from the Type menu.

The type is converted from a PostScript font to a graphic image.

4 Choose Select All from the Edit menu to select all vector graphics (type, circle, and leaves), and copy the selection to the Clipboard.

5 Quit the Adobe Illustrator application and launch the Adobe Photoshop application.

6 With the *09Work.psd* document active, choose New Layer from the pop-up menu in the Layers palette, in the New Layer dialog box enter **Line art layer** in the Name box, and click OK.

7 With the Paths palette open, paste the Adobe Illustrator line art from the Clipboard to the Line art layer, in the Paste dialog box choose the Paste as Paths option, and click OK.

The document window displays the line art paths, and as with Adobe Illustrator it is possible to select an individual subpath and adjust its anchor points or position.

8 Make sure the foreground color is set to black.

9 In the Paths palette click the Fill path icon in the lower-left corner.

10 If necessary, use the move tool to position the line art as shown in the final image.

11 With the Line Art layer selected in the Layers palette, set the Opacity slider to the 50% setting.

12 Save the *09Work.psd* file.

EDITING THE IMAGE

After flattening the image and using the Levels command to reduce the brightness and contrast in the image, you will increase the size of the work canvas to create a white border.

Adjusting the levels

Before adjusting the levels of the image, you must merge or flatten the layers so that adjustments specified in the Levels dialog box are applied to the entire image, not just a single layer.

1 In the Layers palette choose Flatten Image from the Layers palette menu.

2 Double-click the marquee tool, in the Marquee Options palette make sure Rectangular is selected from the Shape pop-up menu, and enter **30** pixels in the Feather box.

3 Drag to select a rectangle about three-quarter inch inside the outer edge of the document.

4 Inverse the selection to select the border.

5 Choose Adjust from the Image menu and Levels from the submenu, in the Levels dialog box make sure the Preview option is selected, enter **0** and **200** in the Output Level boxes to reduce the range of highlights in the image, and click OK.

The document window displays the image with a softer, more even tone.

6 Deselect the rectangular selection.

Adjusting the canvas size

You will increase the work canvas size to add a white border.

1 Choose Canvas Size from the Image menu, in the Canvas Size dialog box, enter **15.25** inches in the Width box and **19.25** inches in the Height box, make sure Placement is set to be center aligned, and click OK.

2 Save the *09Work.psd* file.

PRINTING A NEWSPAPER AD

To print a newspaper advertisement, it would be necessary to establish your Adobe Photoshop file size to equal the final printing size. To determine the optimal resolution of your document, you must first know the halftone screen frequency at which you will be printing. For our purposes, 85 lines per inch (lpi) is satisfactory, and so we double the lpi value to compute the optimal resolution of 170 ppi for our file resolution. For more information on printing, refer to the *Adobe Photoshop User Guide*.

CREATING A BROCHURE COVER

After reducing the size of the image, you will convert the image from Grayscale mode to Duotone mode to create an image to be used for the front cover of a brochure.

Note: Only grayscale images can be converted to duotone images.

Adobe Photoshop allows you to create monotones, duotones, tritones, and quadtones. Monotones are grayscale images printed with a single, nonblack ink. Duotones, tritones, and quadtones are grayscale images printed with two, three, and four inks, respectively. In these types of images, different colored inks are used to reproduce different levels of gray rather than to reproduce different colors.

1 Choose Image Size from the Image menu, and in the Image Size dialog box enter **7** inches in the Width box, without closing the dialog box.

The entire image is automatically proportioned, and the original resolution of 130 ppi is now 283 ppi to compensate for the reduced dimensions of the image.

It is possible to calculate the optimum resolution by doubling the image's line screen setting. This image is set to use the standard line screen setting of 133, so a recommended resolution equals 266 ppi.

2 To re-proportion the entire image to a resolution of 266, deselect the Constrain File Size option in the Image Size box, enter **266** pixels/inch in the Resolution box, and click OK.

3 Choose Save As from the File menu, and when prompted, enter **Brochure.psd** in the Name box, and click Save.

Converting a file to Duotone mode

The use of monotones, duotones, tritones, and quadtones allows you to add dimension and enhance subtle detail in grayscale images. For this example, you will specify a colored ink, producing an image with a tint.

Adobe Photoshop supports PANTONE®* colors for printing inks. Pantone has specified CMYK equivalents for its colors. To select a PANTONE color, determine the ink color you want, using either the PANTONE Color Formula Guide 1000 or an ink chart obtained from your printer.

Note: In Adobe Photoshop, custom colors are printed to their equivalent CMYK plates in every mode except Duotone.

1 With the *Brochure.psd* file active, choose Duotone from the Mode menu, in the Duotone Options dialog box choose Duotone from the Type pop-up menu, and click the Duotone Curve box for Ink 1.

In Duotone mode, you do not have direct access to the individual image channels, such as you do in RGB, CMYK, or Lab modes; instead the channels are manipulated through the curves in the Duotone Curve dialog box.

You can adjust the duotone curve by clicking a point on the graph and dragging, or by entering values for the different ink percentages. The x axis of the curve graph moves from highlights (at the left) to shadows (at the right). The density of the ink increases along the y axis. You can specify up to 13 points on the curve. When you specify two values along the curve, Adobe Photoshop calculates the intermediate values. As you adjust the curve, the values are automatically entered in the percentage text boxes. A value you type in a text box indicates the percentage of the ink color that will be used to print that percentage of the image. For example, if you enter 70 in the 100-percent text box, a 70-percent dot of that ink color will be used to print the 100-percent shadow areas of the image.

Note: To produce fully saturated colors, darker inks should be printed before lighter inks. When entering colors in the duotone dialog boxes, make sure that the inks are specified in descending order; that is, the darkest ink appears at the top, and the lightest ink appears at the bottom. The order of inks affects how Adobe Photoshop applies screens.

2 In the Duotone Curve dialog box (for Ink 1) enter **0**% in the 0 box, **3**% in the 5 box, **30**% in the 50 box, and **95**% in the 100 box, and click OK.

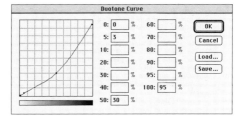

3 In the Duotone Options dialog box click the Duotone Curve box for Ink 2.

4 In the Duotone Curve dialog box (for Ink 2) enter **0**% in the 0 box, **3**% in the 5 box, **35**% in the 50 box, and **80**% in the 100 box, and click OK.

5 In the Duotone Options dialog box select the Color Swatch box for Ink 2 (second white box from the left).

6 Next, in the Custom Colors dialog box choose PANTONE Coated from the Book pop-up menu, type **375** (without pausing) to quickly scroll to the PANTONE 375 CV swatch, and click OK.

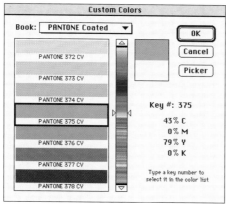

©*Pantone, Inc. 1986, 1993*

Note: *The PANTONE colors in the Adobe Photoshop Custom Color Picker represent the most recent specifications from Pantone, Inc.; therefore some ink names may be slightly different from those in older programs. When you use PANTONE colors in documents that you plan to export to other applications make sure that the Short PANTONE Names option is selected in the More Preferences dialog box. This selection ensures that the PANTONE color names will match the naming convention used in the other applications. If the ink is to be separated on a process color plate, name it "cyan," "magenta," "yellow," or "black."*

7 Save the *Brochure.psd* file.

PRINTING A DUOTONE IMAGE

When creating duotones, keep in mind that both the order in which the inks are printed and the screen angles you use dramatically affect your final output.

Note: *The recommended screen angles and frequencies for quadtones are based on the assumption that Ink 1 is the darkest ink and Ink 4 is the lightest ink.*

In most cases your printer or service bureau will take care of the following details.

1 Choose Page Setup from the File menu, and when prompted, click Screen.

2 In the Halftone Screens dialog box click Auto to set the optimal screen angles and frequencies.

3 In the Auto Screens dialog box click OK.

Note: Be sure to select the Use Accurate Screens option in the Auto Screens dialog box if you're printing to an imagesetter equipped with PostScript Level 2 or an Emerald controller. Low-resolution PostScript Level 2 printers cannot use this option.

4 In the Halftone Screens dialog box click OK, and in the Page Setup dialog box click OK.

5 Choose Save a Copy from the File menu.

When you use the Save a Copy command the file is saved to disk but does not replace or affect the current open file you're working in.

6 When prompted, make sure *Projects* is selected in the pop-up menu, type **Brochure.eps** in the Name box, choose EPS from the Format pop-up menu, and click Save.

7 In the EPS format dialog box click the Include Halftone Screen option, and click OK to make sure the screen information (angles and frequencies) is saved.

8 Close all open files, and quit (or exit) the Adobe Photoshop application.

10

In this project you will incorporate the use of the layering feature and layer masks to create the front panel of a promotional brochure for the German timepiece manu-

PROMOTIONAL BROCHURE

facturer Glock. You will also use the Perspective, Distort, and Skew commands to produce geometrical distortions of selections. ■ The face of the watch is actually a flat stone about ten inches across, and the watch strap is fashioned from steel mesh wrapped around sticks of wood. After photographing a collection of individual objects, such as a Japanese pagoda and a model of the Eiffel tower, we used Adobe Photoshop to scale and place them on the face of the watch, leaving one final object for you to place.

This project features two Adobe Original type-faces, Madrone and Willow. The Madrone typeface, used for the numerals on the watch, was designed by Barbara Lind in 1991. Madrone was digitized from proofs of the wood type collection

PROMOTIONAL BROCHURE

in the National Museum of American History in the Smithsonian Institution in Washington, D. C. A fat face roman, Madrone is typical of popular early nineteenth-century styles. Fat face types are characterized by their squatness and extreme letter width; one familiar version of this design is Bodoni Ultra Bold. Madrone is eye-catching for display uses in advertising and packaging.

Willow, designed in 1990 by Joy Redick, is a condensed typeface modeled on nineteenth-century wood types known as Clarendons (wood type Clarendons do not resemble the English metal types of that name). Clarendon condensed faces were originally so well-designed that words or a line of display type have an even color that is remarkable for wood types. Taken from proofs of type in the Rob Roy Kelly Collection housed at the University of Texas at Austin, Willow can be used for display work such as packaging, advertising, and posters.

This project covers:

• Using the burn tool

• Adding layer masks

• Turning off a layer mask

• Merging layers

• Using the Levels command to increase the brightness and contrast in a selection

• Using the layers feature to create a precision drop shadow

• Using the Perspective command, the Distort command, and the Skew command.

It should take you about 90 minutes to complete this project.

Viewing the final image

1 Before launching the Adobe Photoshop application, throw away the Adobe Photoshop Preferences file to make sure all settings are returned to their default values.

2 Make sure the Madrone and Willow fonts, found on the *Advanced Adobe Photoshop* CD-ROM disc, are installed.

3 Launch the Adobe Photoshop application, and open the *10Final.psd* file in *10Project* to view the final image.

4 Reduce the view of the *10Final.psd* document, and drag it to the upper-right corner of your desktop to use as a visual reference.

Opening an Adobe Photoshop file

Rather than creating a new file, you will open the existing Adobe Photoshop document, *Watch.psd*.

1 Open the *Watch.psd* file in *10Project*.

The watch image was scanned from a 4-by-5 transparency on a Leafscan 45 transparency scanner at a resolution of 300 dpi. For the sake of reducing the demand for disk space on your system, you will work with a file resolution of 72 dpi.

2 Save the *Watch.psd* file as *10Work.psd* to *Projects*.

PLACING AND EDITING IMAGES

After placing and editing the recliner image, you will merge the layers before placing the painting image. And then, after placing the painting image, you will edit and apply a layer mask that allows only unmasked portions of the painting image to be viewable.

Placing the recliner image

After copying the recliner image from the *10Work.psd* file to your working document, you will scale and position the image.

1 Open the *10Lib.psd* file in *10Project*, and select the Recliner layer in the Layers palette, hiding the Painting layer.

The document window displays the recliner image on a transparent background.

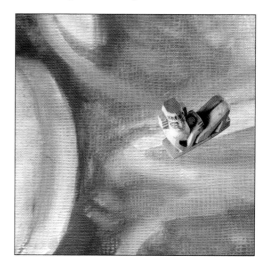

2 With the move tool selected, drag the Recliner layer from the Layers palette of the *10Lib.psd* file to the document window of the *10Work.psd* file.

The Layers palette for the *10Work.psd* file displays the Recliner layer, and the document window displays the recliner image.

3 With the Info palette displayed and with the Recliner layer selected in the Layers palette, choose Effects from the Image menu and Scale from the submenu.

TIP: TO TOGGLE BE-
TWEEN THE DODGE/
BURN/SPONGE TOOL,
HOLD DOWN THE OP-
TION KEY (OR ALT KEY)
AND CLICK THE TOOL
IN THE TOOLBOX.

4 Hold down the Shift key (to maintain a proportional scale), and drag one of the handles to reduce the recliner image until the Info palette indicates the image is about 75% of its original size.

5 Drag in the document window to position the recliner image in the six o'clock position on the face of the watch image as shown in the illustration below.

6 Save the *10Work.psd* file.

Airbrushing a drop shadow

You will create a drop shadow behind the Recliner image by choosing the Behind mode from the Airbrush Options palette. Behind mode works only in layers that contain transparency. When you apply paint, it appears that you are painting on the *back* of the transparent areas in a sheet of acetate.

Note: It is not possible to choose Behind mode for the Background layer or for a floating selection.

1 With Recliner layer selected in the Layers palette, double-click the airbrush tool, in the Airbrush Options palette choose Behind from the Mode pop-up menu, and set the Pressure slider to 10%.

2 In the Brushes palette select a 13-pixel, soft-edged brush.

3 Paint along the top edge of the *Recliner* image to create the drop shadow.

Darkening the recliner image using the burn tool

You will darken the lower edge of the recliner image using the burn tool. The burn tool and the dodge tool are based on the traditional photographer's technique of increasing the amount of exposure given to a specific area on a print. Photographers increase the exposure to darken areas on a print (burning-in) or hold back light during an exposure to lighten an area on the print (dodging).

1 Press the Caps Lock key to select the precision tool cursor.

2 With Recliner layer selected in the Layers palette, double-click the dodge/burn/sponge tool in the toolbox, in the Toning Tools Options palette make sure Midtones is selected in the Mode pop-up menu and the Exposure is set to 10%, and choose Burn from the Tool pop-up menu.

Note: The Midtones mode limits any modification to the middle range of colors.

3 Using the selected 13-pixel, soft-edged brush, paint along the front and lower edges of the recliner image to darken the image as shown in the illustration below, experimenting with shadows and highlights if you wish.

Merging layers

Assuming you have finalized the characteristics and positioning of the image, you will merge the two existing layers to create an intermediate version of your document, reducing the size of the *10Work.psd* file.

1 In the Layers palette make sure both layers are displayed (eye icons visible), make sure one of the layers to be merged is selected, and choose Merge Layers from the Layers palette menu.

All visible layers are merged into the background layer.

Placing the painting image

After copying the painting image from the *10Lib.psd* file to your working document, you will position and scale the image to fill the entire work canvas.

The painting image is a painted canvas that was scanned on a flatbed scanner at a scan resolution of 200 dpi. You will use this image to apply an overall texture to the background of the watch image.

1 Open the *10Lib.psd* file, and select the Painting layer in the Layers palette, hiding the Recliner layer.

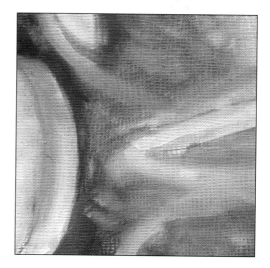

2 Drag the Painting layer from the Layers palette of the *10Lib.psd* file to the document window of the *10Work.psd* file.

The Layers palette of the *10Work.psd* file displays the Painting layer, and the document window displays the painting image.

TIP: TO FILL A SELEC-
TION WITH THE FORE-
GROUND COLOR, HOLD
DOWN THE OPTION KEY
(OR ALT KEY) AND PRESS
THE DELETE KEY.

3 With the Painting layer selected in the Layers palette, drag to align the upper-left corner of the painting image with the upper-left corner of the work canvas.

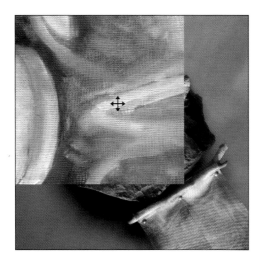

4 With the Painting layer selected in the Layers palette, choose Effects from the Image menu and Scale from the submenu, drag the lower-right handle to the lower-right corner of the window, and click the gavel icon to confirm the scale.

5 Close the *10Lib.psd* file.

Adding a layer mask

As you have seen in previous projects, a layer mask is a viewing option that lets you experiment with revealing parts of a layer, without actually altering the pixel information on the layer itself.

1 With the Painting layer selected in the Layers palette, choose Add Layer Mask from the Layers palette menu.

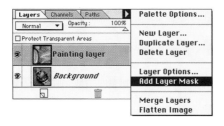

The Painting layer in the Layers palette displays a mask thumbnail to the right of the layer thumbnail. The dark outline around the mask thumbnail indicates the layer mask is the target for editing on the Painting layer.

Note: Click either the layer thumbnail or the mask thumbnail to select a target for editing on a layer.

2 In the Layers palette make sure the mask thumbnail is selected in the Painting layer, and choose All from the Select menu.

3 Fill the layer mask with black, temporarily "masking" the painting image on the Painting layer as if it were transparent.

The Layers palette displays the mask thumbnail as solid black, and the document window displays the image on the Painting layer to be completely masked (or transparent).

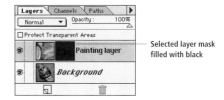

Selected layer mask
filled with black

4 Click the switch color icon in the toolbox to set the foreground color to white.

You will paint with white on the layer mask to unmask portions of the painting image, making some of it viewable.

5 Double-click the airbrush tool, in the Airbrush Options palette choose Normal from the Mode pop-up menu, and set the Pressure slider to 50%.

6 In the Brushes palette select a soft-edged brush.

7 In the Layers palette make sure the mask thumbnail is selected in the Painting layer.

TIP: HOLD DOWN THE COMMAND KEY (OR CTRL KEY), AND CLICK THE MASK THUMBNAIL IN THE LAYERS PALETTE TO TOGGLE BETWEEN TURNING THE LAYER MASK ON AND OFF.

8 In the document window of the *10Work.psd* file paint over portions of the blue background to erase portions of the layer mask, unmasking portions of the painting image.

The document window displays a slightly mottled effect in the background.

Turning off the layer mask

As you have seen, all editing to a layer mask is displayed in the document window. If you want to view the layer without the layer mask, you can temporarily turn it off.

Note: To remove a layer mask, drag the mask thumbnail to the Trash icon at the bottom of the Layers palette.

1 In the Layers palette double-click the mask thumbnail on the Painting layer, in the Layer Mask Options dialog box click Do Not Apply to Layer, and click OK.

The document window displays the entire painting image, and the Layers palette displays a red X over the mask thumbnail.

2 In the Layers palette click the mask thumbnail to reapply the layer mask.

Merging layers

You will merge all layers into the Background layer using the Merge Layers command. Although it is possible to use the Flatten Image command to merge all layers, you may wish to use the Flatten Image command with discretion since layers not displayed are discarded.

1 In the Layers palette make sure all layers are displayed, make sure one of the layers is selected, and choose Merge Layers from the Layers palette menu.

The Layers palette no longer displays the mask thumbnail for the Painting layer, indicating the layer mask was automatically applied to the Painting layer when the layers were merged.

2 Deselect everything, and save the *10Work.psd* file.

EDITING THE BORDER

You will use the Gaussian Blur filter, the Invert command, and the Levels command to edit the border of the image.

Applying the Gaussian Blur filter

After applying the Gaussian Blur filter to the selected border, you will select a smaller border within the first border and use the Invert command to invert the selected border.

1 Double-click the marquee tool, in the Marquee Options palette choose Rectangular from the Shape pop-up menu, choose Fixed Size from the Style pop-up menu, and enter **416** pixels in the Width box, **396** pixels in the Height box, and **9** pixels in the Feather box.

2 Click the document window, hold down the mouse button, and drag to center the selection marquee in the work canvas.

3 Inverse the selection to select the border.

4 Choose Blur from the Filter menu and Gaussian Blur from the submenu, in the Gaussian Blur dialog box enter **2** pixels in the Radius box, and click OK.

5 Deselect the border.

Using the Invert command

After selecting the border, you will use the Invert command to invert the colors of the border. The Invert command creates a negative of an image. You might use this command to turn a positive into a negative or to create a positive image from a scanned negative.

To further edit the border, you will use the Levels command to adjust the brightness and contrast of the selection.

Note: When you invert an image, the brightness value of each pixel in the channels is converted to the inverse value on the 256-step color value scale. For example, a pixel in a positive image with a pixel value of 255 is changed to 0, and a pixel with a value of 5 is changed to 250.

1 Double-click the marquee tool, in the Marquee Options palette make sure Rectangular is selected from the Shape pop-up menu and Fixed Size is selected from the Style pop-up menu, and enter **470** pixels in the Width box, **450** pixels in the Height box, and **0** pixels in the Feather box.

2 Click the document window, hold down the mouse button, and drag to center the selection marquee in the work canvas.

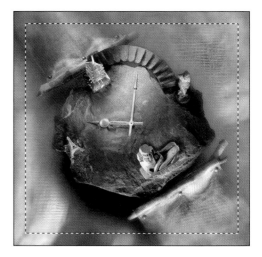

3 Inverse the selection to select the border.

4 Choose Map from the Image menu and Invert from the submenu to invert the colors in the selection.

Using the Levels command

The Levels command allows you to make gradual adjustments to the brightness, contrast, and gamma in an image.

1 Choose Adjust from the Image menu and Levels from the submenu.

The Levels dialog box displays a histogram of the image. The histogram plots the brightness values versus the number of pixels at each level. The darkest pixels appear at the left; the brightest pixels appear at the right.Input Levels shows the current values; Output Levels indicates the desired output values.

2 In the Levels dialog box click the Preview option, enter **28**, **1.00**, and **217** in the Input Levels boxes, enter **0** and **210** in the Output Levels boxes, and click OK.

3 Deselect the border.

CREATING A PRECISION DROP SHADOW

With the layering feature it's easier than ever to create a drop shadow. In this example, after placing the four numbers on a layer to create the drop shadow image, you will duplicate the drop shadow layer, and then edit the duplicated drop shadow image to create the numbers themselves.

Placing the number 8

After placing the type, adjusting the perspective of the image, and rotating the image, you will create a layer for the drop shadow image.

1 With the foreground color set to black, select the type tool, click the image, in the Type Tool dialog box choose Madrone from the Font pop-up menu, enter **120** points in the Size box, type **8** in the text box, and click OK.

2 With the move tool selected, drag in the document window to position the number '8' in the eight o'clock position on the face of the watch image.

3 Choose Effects from the Image menu and Perspective from the submenu.

The Perspective command allows you to create a three-dimensional effect by moving two handles in opposite directions at the same time.

4 Drag the upper-left handle up and drag the upper-right handle down.

Note: *When you drag a handle, the opposing handle moves as well.*

TIP: DOUBLE-CLICK A
FLOATING SELECTION IN
THE LAYERS PALETTE TO
MAKE A NEW LAYER.

5 Click the gavel icon to confirm the selection.

6 Choose Rotate from the Image menu and Arbitrary from the submenu, in the Arbitrary Rotate dialog box enter **50°** in the Angle box, click the CCW (counterclockwise) option, and click OK.

7 In the Layers palette drag the Floating Selection to the New Layer icon in the lower-left corner, in the Make Layer dialog box type **Drop Shadow layer** in the Name box, and click OK.

8 Deselect the type, and save the *10Work.psd* file.

Placing the number 5

After positioning the type, you will distort the image.

1 With the type tool selected, click the image, in the Type Tool dialog box make sure Madrone is selected from the Font pop-up menu, enter **60** points in the Size box, type **5** in the text box, and click OK.

2 With the move tool selected, drag in the document window to position the number '5' in the five o'clock position on the face of the watch image.

3 Choose Effects from the Image menu and Distort from the submenu.

The Distort command allows you to drag each handle independently.

4 Drag the upper-right handle up and to the right about ¼ inch and drag the lower-right handle down and to the right about ¼ inch.

5 Click the gavel icon to confirm the distortion, and deselect the type.

Placing the number 2

After positioning the type, you will skew the image.

1 With the type tool selected, click the image, in the Type Tool dialog box type **2** in the text box, and click OK.

2 With the move tool selected, drag in the document window to position the number '2' in the two o'clock position on the face of the watch image.

3 Choose Effects from the Image menu and Skew from the submenu.

The Skew command allows you to slant a selection vertically or horizontally along the edge of the selection.

4 Drag the upper-right handle up.

5 Click the gavel icon to confirm the scale, and deselect the type.

Placing the number 10

After adjusting the perspective of the type, you will rotate it.

1 With the type tool selected, click the image, in the Type Tool dialog box enter **40** points in the Size box, type **10** in the text box, and click OK.

2 With the move tool selected, drag in the document window to position the number '10' in the ten o'clock position on the face of the watch.

3 Choose Effects from the Image menu and Perspective from the submenu.

4 Drag the upper-right handle down and left about ⅛ inch and drag the upper-left handle up and left about ⅛ inch.

5 Click the gavel icon to confirm the scale.

6 Choose Rotate from the Image menu and Arbitrary from the submenu, in the Arbitrary Rotate dialog box enter **13°** in the Angle box, click the CW (clockwise) option, and click OK.

7 Deselect the type, and save the *10Work.psd* file.

PLACING THE NUMBERS

After duplicating the Drop shadow layer and using the Invert command to convert the image from black to white, you will drag the entire duplicated layer so that the drop shadows are visible.

1 In the Layers palette drag the Drop shadow layer to the New Layer icon in the lower-left corner.

2 Double-click the Drop shadow layer copy, in the Layer Options dialog box enter **Type layer** in the Name box, and click OK.

3 Choose Map from the Image menu and Invert from the submenu to cause the numbers to be inverted from black to white.

4 With the Type layer selected in the Layers palette and with the move tool selected, drag the entire Type layer in the document window up and right approximately ¼ inch.

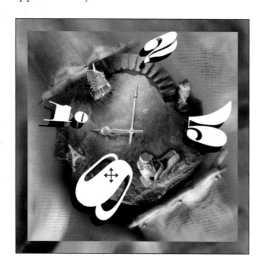

5 With Drop shadow layer selected in the Layers palette, choose Blur from the Filter menu and Gaussian Blur from the submenu, in the Gaussian Blur dialog box type **4** pixels in the Radius box, and click OK.

6 In the Layers palette select the Drop shadow layer, and set the Opacity slider to 75%.

7 In the Layers palette select the Type layer, and set the Opacity slider in the Layers palette to 60%.

8 Save the *10Work.psd* file.

Merging the layers

Again, for the sake of reducing the size of the document, merge the layers.

1 With all layers visible (eye icons displayed for each layer), choose Merge Layers from the Layers palette menu.

2 Save the *10Work.psd* file.

CREATING THE GLOCK LOGO

It's easy to create a layer mask with type. In this example, after adding a layer mask to the Logo layer, you will place the type on the layer mask itself. As a result, wherever the type masks the blue logo image, the background image can be seen.

Placing the blue logo

You will place the logo image on a layer of its own.

1 In the Layers palette click the New Layer icon in the lower-left corner, in the New Layer dialog box enter **Logo layer** in the Name box, and click OK.

2 Double-click the marquee tool, in the Marquee Options palette choose Elliptical from the Shape pop-up menu and Fixed Size from the Style menu, and enter **117** pixels in the Width box and **117** pixels in the Height box.

3 Click the upper-right corner of the document window to create a circle and drag it to position it.

4 Click the foreground color swatch in the toolbox, and in the Color Picker dialog box enter the following settings:

    Red..................30
    Green 44
    Blue...............138

5 Click OK to set the foreground color to blue.

6 Fill the circle with blue.

7 Deselect the circle, and save the *10Work.psd* file.

Adding a layer mask

After adding a layer mask, you will edit it by placing the GLOCK type on the layer mask itself.

1 With Logo layer selected in the Layers palette, choose Add Layer Mask from the Layers palette menu.

2 In the Layers palette make sure the mask thumbnail is selected in the Logo layer.

3 Click the default colors icon to set the foreground color to black.

4 With the type tool selected, click the circle, in the Type Tool dialog box choose Willow from the Font pop-up menu, enter **90** points in the Size box, type **GLOCK** in uppercase letters in the text box, and click OK.

5 Drag to center the type in the circle.

6 Deselect the type, and save the *10Work.psd* file.

7 Close all open files, and quit (or exit) the Adobe Photoshop application.

EASTERN
STYLE

11

In this project you will color correct an image that is to be the front cover of a magazine using the improved production controls that come with

HIGH FASHION MAGAZINE

Adobe Photoshop 3.0. These powerful new tools include the Selective Color command that lets you adjust the ink amounts of individual color channels or plates. The new Replace Color command enables you to create masks based on specific colors, and then correct the color by adjusting the hue, saturation, and brightness values. ■ After using the new Gamut Warning command to highlight the areas in the image that are out of the CMYK gamut, you will use the new CMYK Preview command to display the image in CMYK mode without going through a full mode conversion. You will also use the new sponge tool to desaturate color in an image area with a soft-edged brush.

Both fonts used in this project are taken from the Adobe Original typefaces, Viva and Willow. Viva, designed by Carol Twombly, was released in 1993 as the first open-face design in the Adobe Originals Library. Viva is a multiple master typeface

HIGH FASHION MAGAZINE

with weight and width axes that allow variations of Viva to be generated by the user. Viva's weight axis can be thought of as a shadow axis: as the weight increases, the design casts a longer shadow in a weight range from light to bold. Viva's width axis ranges from condensed to extra-extended. The display possibilities are essentially unlimited; the generated variations allow for legible copyfitting in advertising, book titles, posters, and any display material that needs an original look.

Willow, designed in 1990 by Joy Redick, is a condensed typeface modeled on nineteenth-century wood types known as Clarendons (wood type Clarendons do not resemble the English metal types of that name). Clarendon condensed faces were originally so well-designed that words or a line of display type have an even color that is remarkable for wood types. Taken from proofs of type in the Rob Roy Kelly Collection housed at the University of Texas at Austin, Willow can be used for display work such as packaging, advertising, and posters.

In this project, you will color correct in a specific order that may work well in your own projects. As you execute the project, bear in mind that it is likely that other approaches to this scenario exist.

This project covers:

• Checking the quality of a scan

• Identifying the image key type using the Histogram command

• Setting the black (shadows)and white (highlights) points in the Levels dialog box

• Adjusting midtones with the Curves dialog box

• Displaying out-of-gamut colors

• Correcting out-of-gamut colors with the sponge tool

• Converting a document to CMYK mode

• Using the Replace Color command

• Applying the Unsharp Mask filter and the Gaussian Blur filter

• Using the Dust & Scratches filter

• Using the rubber stamp tool.

It should take you about 2 hours to complete this project.

Viewing the final image

1 Before launching the Adobe Photoshop application, throw away the Adobe Photoshop Preferences to ensure all settings are returned to their default values.

2 Make sure the Viva and Willow fonts, found on the *Advanced Adobe Photoshop* CD-ROM disc, are installed.

3 Launch the Adobe Photoshop application, and open the *11Final.psd* file in *11Project*.

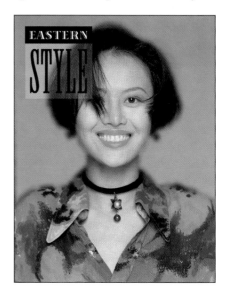

The final image shows deep, rich tones. We deliberately created the blurred edge around the model. Reduce the view of the *11Final.psd* document, and position the final image in the upper-right corner of your monitor to use it as a visual reference.

Opening the original scanned image
1 Open the *Model.psd* file in *11Project*.

The original photograph you will use was scanned on a Leafscan 45 transparency scanner at a resolution of 300 dpi. For the sake of reducing the demand for disk space on your system, you will execute this project at a resolution of 72 ppi.

2 Save the *Model.psd* file as *11Work.psd* to *Projects*.

COLOR CORRECTION
The key to good color reproduction is to produce an image with proper tonal balance (correct brightness, saturation, contrast, and density range) and good color balance, meaning the image has true neutral gray and no color casts.

You will execute a recommended procedure for making color corrections. In general, it may not be necessary to perform each step, depending on the image and the goal to be achieved.

Note: If you have not calibrated your entire system (including the scanner, imagesetter, and workstation), you must color correct numerically using target CMYK values.

CHECKING THE QUALITY OF THE SCAN
It is difficult, if not impossible, to achieve good final output if image details are not captured during scanning. To make sure that minimal color information has been lost in the scanning process, it is a good idea to check the pixel values of your highlight and shadow areas after scanning.

Note: Scan a gray wedge with your image so that you can easily detect and correct a color cast introduced by scanning.

Before scanning, it is best to determine the correct resolution. If you are not sure of your final output size or resolution, it is a good idea to scan the image at a higher resolution than you need for your output, and then resample the image later.

Note: Refer to the Adobe Photoshop User Guide *for more information on determining the correct scan resolution.*

1 With the Info palette open, in the document window of the *11Work.psd* file move the cursor over the lightest highlight areas in the image, and note the values that appear in the Info palette.

For the highlights, the RGB values should read from about 240 to 255.

2 Move the cursor over the darkest shadow areas in the image, and note the values that appear in the Info palette.

For the shadows, the RGB values should read from about 10 to 25.

Overall, it seems our image contains a tonal range that encompasses enough detail to produce good results.

Identifying an image key type

Before you begin making color corrections, it is useful to identify the image key type of the image you are working with. Images can be classified into three key types depending on the visual distribution of tones within the image.

Whereas light images have predominately light tones (high key) and dark images have a majority of dark tones (low key), average images have equal amounts of light and dark tones.

Identifying the key type (determining where the detail is in the image) helps you make correct decisions when you are adjusting brightness and contrast.

1 Choose Histogram from the Image menu.

The Histogram dialog box displays a graphic representation of the tonal distribution (the brightness and darkness levels) in an image. The x axis represents the color values from darkest (0) to brightest (255) at the far right. The y axis represents the total number of pixels with that value.

The numerical values at the lower left of the Histogram dialog box display statistical information about the color values of the pixels:

• Mean is the average brightness value.

• Standard deviation (Std Dev) represents how widely the values vary.

• Median shows the middle value in the range of color values.

• Pixels represents the total number of pixels in the image or selected area.

A histogram representing a low key image shows most of the pixels to the left, and a high key image shows more pixels to the right.

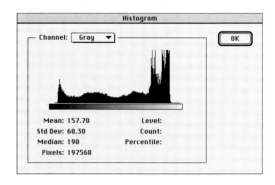

This particular histogram indicates the image almost completely covers the range of values from light to dark, with many pixels in the highlight area.

2 Click OK to close the Histogram dialog box.

Note: The histogram is for information only; you don't make any adjustments using the Histogram command.

Adjusting highlights to be neutral

After using the Levels dialog box in Threshold mode to identify the highlights in the image, you will assign a typical printable neutral white value to the highlights.

1 Double-click the eyedropper tool, and in the Eyedropper Options palette choose 3 by 3 Average from the Sample Size pop-up menu.

Note: The 3 by 3 average ensures your adjustments are based on a true sample of the area you click rather than an individual pixel value.

2 Choose Adjust from the Image menu and Levels from the submenu.

The Levels dialog box displays a histogram of the image. As you have just seen, the histogram plots the brightness values versus the number of pixels at each level. The Input values show the current values; the Output Levels indicate the desired output values.

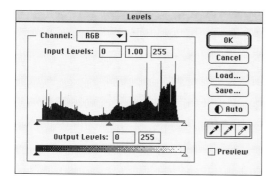

You can use the Levels dialog box in Threshold mode to find the highlight and shadow areas in your image.

3 In the Levels dialog box make sure the Preview option is not selected, hold down the Option key (or Alt key) and slowly drag the right Input slider to the center of the histogram to identify the light areas in the image.

The image changes to Threshold mode. As you drag the Input slider to the left, the model's teeth and other areas that appear first are the lightest areas in the image.

4 Make sure the right Input slider is positioned about at color value 242 (where the lightest areas begin to appear).

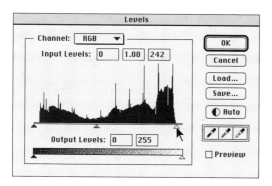

5 In the Levels dialog box, double-click the white eyedropper tool (right-most tool), in the Color Picker dialog box enter the following settings, and click OK.

Cyan 5%
Magenta 3%
Yellow 3%
Black 0%

Note: A typical printable white is created by the CMY percentages of 5, 3, and 3.

6 In the document window click the model's teeth (or another portion of the lightest areas) to set those pixel values in the image to the new white value.

Choosing a white color in the image, rather than a true highlight, can result in loss of detail in the highlights.

Note: For average and high key type images use the 5, 3, and 3 white value. For low key images, enter a white value of 7, 3, and 3 to darken the highlight and hold the detail in the paper. For images that contain very burned-out white, try using even higher values.

The yellow color cast is reduced with the new white value assigned to the highlights.

Adjusting shadows to be neutral

Again, using the Levels dialog box in Threshold mode to identify the shadows in the image, you will assign a target shadow value to the shadow areas in the image.

7 In the Levels dialog box make sure the Preview option is not selected, hold down the Option key (or Alt key) and slowly drag the left Input slider to the center of the histogram to identify the dark areas in the image.

The image changes to Threshold mode. As you drag the Input slider to the left, the portions of the model's hair and other areas that appear first are the darkest areas in the image.

8 Make sure the left Input slider is positioned about at color value 12 (where the darkest areas begin to appear).

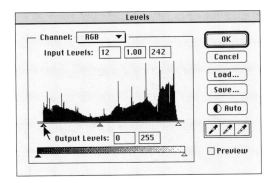

9 In the Levels dialog box, double-click the black eyedropper tool (left-most tool), in the Color Picker dialog box enter the following settings, and click OK.

Cyan 65%
Magenta..... 53%
Yellow 51%
Black 95%

Note: A typical target shadow value is created by the CMYK percentages of 65, 53, 51, and 95.Click the darker portions of the model's hair to set those pixel values to the new shadow value.

10 In the document window click the darkest portions of model's hair (or another portion of the darkest areas) to set those pixel values in the image to the new shadow value.

11 Click OK to close the Levels dialog box.

Adjusting the midtones

You are ready to use the Curves dialog box to fine-tune the contrast in the image by adjusting the midtones.

Like the Levels dialog box, the Curves dialog box lets you adjust the tonal range of an image. However, instead of making the adjustments using just three variables (highlights, shadows, and gamma), you can adjust any point along the gray-level scale while keeping up to 15 other values constant.

For some images, this step may not be necessary; setting the white and black points is often the only contrast adjustment needed. For our image, it will work best to increase the tonal range in the highlight areas on the model's skin.

Note: Refer to the Adobe Photoshop User Guide *for information on fine-tuning the tonal range.*

1 Choose Adjust from the Image menu and Curves from the submenu.

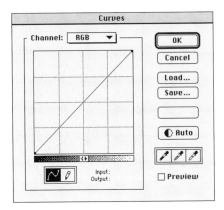

By default the Curves dialog box displays the curve as a diagonal line moving from shadows on the left to highlights on the right, and the output and input values match RGB values. The x axis represents the original brightness values of the pixels, from 0 to 255 (input levels); the y axis represents the new brightness values (output levels). For this reason, the diagonal line represents the current relationship; every pixel has the same input and output levels.

2 Click the arrow in the bar under the graph to reverse the direction of the grayscale and display the input and output values in percentages to match the CMYK values.

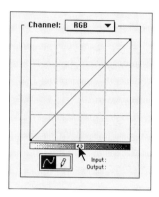

The grayscale bar shows white on the left to black on the right.

3 Hold down the mouse button, and drag the eye-dropper in the document window to find the corresponding values on the graph.

A circle appears to mark a pixel's position on the graph in the Curves dialog box, and the Input and Output values are displayed at the bottom of the dialog box.

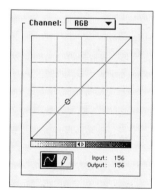

4 Drag the eyedropper in the document window over the lightest areas on the model's skin to find its brightness values on the graph.

The highlights are represented in the lower-left portion of the graph. Knowing that you may wish to make specific adjustments to these highlights,

you can add points to the curve, allowing you to isolate adjustments to the highlights and not affect the shadows.

5 In the Curves dialog box position the cursor on the graph at Input value 40% and Output value 40% and click to create a point on the graph.

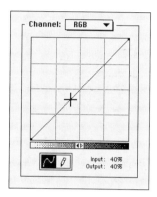

Note: Rather than add a point at Input value 25% and Output value 25% on the graph, we have allowed for a smoother, more gradual adjustment to the highlights by adding the point at 40% and 40%.

6 Position the cursor on the graph to the left of the newly added point, and drag the graph up or down.

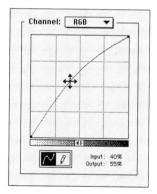

The portion to the right of the point moves in the reverse direction.

Note: To remove a point, drag it off the graph.

7 To isolate adjustments to the highlights, click another anchor point at Input value 50% and Output value 50%.

8 Again, drag the left portion of the graph up or down to see how the right portion is now isolated.

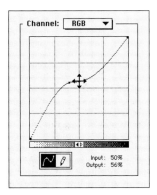

WINDOWS PLATFORM:

RENAME ALL ✶.HSS

FILES TO ✶.AHU.

RENAME ALL ✶.CRV

FILES TO ✶.ACV.

9 When you are finished experimenting with adjusting the tonal range, click the Load button in the Curves dialog box, and when prompted, choose *Curve01.crv* in *11Project*, and click the Open button.

The Curves dialog box displays the stored settings, and the document window displays how the overall saturation of the image is increased.

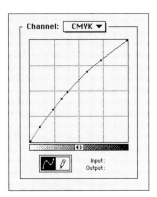

10 In the Curves dialog box click OK, and save the *11Work.psd* file.

Intensifying the background color

Before converting to the RGB image to CMYK mode, you will use the Replace Color command to intensify the green background color. The Replace Color command lets you create a mask based on specific colors and then adjust the hue, saturation, and lightness values to correct the color. Unlike

that created with the Color Mask command, however, the mask is temporary and does not create a selection in the image. The mask is used only to replace color.

1 Choose Adjust from the Image menu and Replace Color from the submenu.

The Replace Color dialog box contains a preview box you can use to see the mask you're creating or to see a copy of the entire image. In most cases, you will want to leave the preview set to Selection so you can view the mask as you build it. Change the preview box to Image when you want to add to the mask but the area you want to select is not visible in the original image. For example, you might not be able to see the entire image when you're working in a magnified view or when the dialog box is covering part of the document window. Reselect the Mask option to see the effect of any changes to the mask.

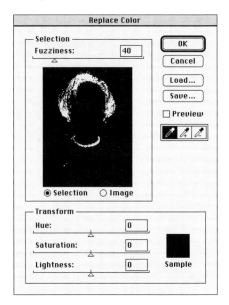

2 In the Replace Color dialog box click the Preview option (to view the results in the Preview window), enter **25** in the Fuzziness box, make sure the Selection option is selected, and click the green background in the document window.

The Preview window displays the selected portions of the image in white.

3 To select the background more thoroughly, click the plus eyedropper and click the unselected portions of the background (black portions) in the Preview window several more times until most of the background is selected as shown in the illustration below.

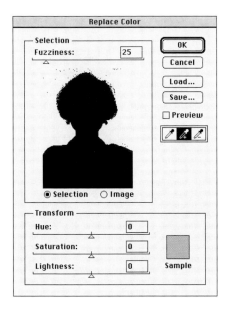

4 In the Replace Color dialog box enter **25** in the Hue box, **51** in the Saturation box, and **-25** in the Lightness box, and click OK.

The green background color is darker and more saturated with color.

Before   *After*

Displaying out-of-gamut colors

You will use the Gamut Warning command to view which portions of this RGB image are not in the CMYK gamut.

The gamut of a color system is the range of colors that can be displayed or printed in that system. An out-of-gamut color refers to a color that may exist in the RGB and HSB color models, but it does not exist in the CMYK gamut and, therefore, cannot be printed.

Note: When you are working in RGB mode and select or pass the cursor over an out-of-gamut color, an alert triangle with an exclamation point appears in the Picker palette or the Color Picker dialog box. An exclamation point appears next to the CMYK values in the Info palette. The Picker palette and the Color Picker dialog box display the closest CMYK equivalent below the triangle. If you wish to select the CMYK equivalent, click the triangle.

1 To recognize non-printable, out-of-gamut colors, choose Gamut Warning from the Mode menu.

Adobe Photoshop builds a color conversion table (based on the calibration settings) and identifies the out-of-gamut colors by displaying them as gray.

Depending on the colors in your image, you may want to change the gamut warning color. Since the out-of-gamut warning color is quite similar to some of the gray tones that appear in the model's blouse, you will change the warning color to light blue.

2 Choose Preferences in the File menu and Gamut Warning in the submenu, and in the Gamut Warning dialog box click the Color swatch.

3 In the Color Picker dialog box enter the following settings:

Cyan 52%
Magenta 0%
Yellow 25%
Black.............0%

4 Click OK to close the Color Picker dialog box, and click OK to close the Gamut Warning Preferences dialog box.

Adobe Photoshop replaces the default out-of-gamut warning color with a light blue color.

5 Choose Gamut Warning from the Mode menu to turn off the warning.

Previewing the image in CMYK mode

Knowing that portions of the image are out-of-gamut, it's a good idea to check to see if converting to CMYK produces satisfactory colors.

Prior to actually converting the image to CMYK mode, it is possible to preview CMYK color values using the CMYK Preview command. Remember that since the image is previewed in CMYK mode, all previewed colors are, by definition, in the CMYK gamut and printable.

1 Choose CMYK Preview from the Mode menu.

The image is displayed in CMYK mode, and by definition, all colors displayed are in-gamut.

Note: Depending on your monitor calibration and system calibration, you may or may not have any indication of an out-of gamut condition.

A CMYK preview gives you the choice of whether or not you wish to make further adjustments to the color before you convert to CMYK mode.

Note: Adobe Photoshop does not perform an actual conversion; instead, the Adobe Photoshop application temporarily displays colors in their CMYK equivalent, an advantage if you have enough RAM for a three-channel RGB image, but not enough RAM for a four-channel CMYK image.

Correcting an out-of-gamut color

Even though converting an image to CMYK mode means all colors are in the CMYK gamut and printable, you may wish to correct some out-of-gamut colors yourself. For example, if you were not satisfied with the color of the model's mouth in the CMYK preview, you could experiment with correcting the color in RGB mode to see if you can get more desirable results.

In this example you will use the sponge tool to desaturate the color of the model's mouth. The sponge tool makes it possible to add or subtract saturation from small, contiguous areas in an image.

Note: Refer to the Adobe Photoshop User Guide for information on color correcting in distinct out-of-gamut areas that contain relatively pure color with defined edges, such as logos, swatches, filled areas, or areas painted using Normal mode.

Time out for a movie

If your system is capable of running Adobe Teach movies, you can see a preview of the technique that shows how to use the sponge tool to desaturate out-of-gamut areas in an image that is covered in this section. Play the movie named Gamut Warning. For information on how to play Adobe Teach movies, see the "What You Need To Do" section at the beginning of this book.

1 Choose Gamut Warning from the Mode menu.

2 Double-click the dodge/burn/sponge tool, in the Toning Tools Options palette choose the Sponge from the Tool pop-up menu, make sure Desaturate is selected in the Mode pop-up menu, and set the Pressure slider to 20%.

3 In the Brushes palette select the 17-pixel, soft-edged brush (fourth from the right in the second row).

4 For a quick preview as you adjust out-of-gamut colors, open an additional window by choosing the New Window command in the Window menu.

Without the warning in the reference window, you can monitor the changes made to the image.

5 Hold down the Caps Lock key (to display the sponge cursor as a crosshair), and make smooth, even sweeps over the portions of the model's mouth that are out-of-gamut, allowing just a trace of the out-of-gamut mask to remain since too much sponging can make the color muddy or cause streaks in painted areas.

As the colors become less saturated, they come into the CMYK gamut, and the warning color disappears. Because Photoshop brings the color into gamut during the CMYK conversion, it may not be necessary to eliminate the entire gamut warning to get the results you want. Monitor the CMYK color in the second window; as soon as you are satisfied with the color in this window, save the image.

We'll assume the remaining out-of-gamut regions look okay in the CMYK preview, so it won't be necessary to adjust them.

6 Choose Gamut Warning from the Mode menu to turn off gamut warning.

7 Save the *11Work.psd* file, and close the *New Window* document.

Converting the image to CMYK mode

Converting an RGB image to CMYK mode splits the RGB colors into the four colors commonly used for printing color separations: cyan, magenta, yellow, and black. It's not a good idea to convert between RGB and CMYK mode multiple times, because each time the image is converted, the color values must be recalculated.

1 Choose CMYK Color from the Mode menu.

The image is converted to CMYK mode.

Adjusting color casts

It's usually best to adjust or eliminate any color casts in an image after you have converted the image to CMYK mode. In this example, you will identify the channel or channels that hold the most color information, and then adjust the brightness and contrast using the Curves dialog box with the identified channels as the target.

1 With the Info palette open, drag over the image to see which channels (CMYK) have the highest percentages.

The Info palette indicates the image has high percentages of magenta and yellow.

2 In the Channels palette click the Magenta channel, hold down the Shift key, click the Yellow channel to select both channels to be the target, and click the left-most column of the CMYK channel to display it (eye icon visible).

3 Choose Adjust from the Image menu and Curves from the submenu.

As you have seen before, the Curves dialog box displays the graph showing the relationship between input and output levels. Directly below the graph, the grayscale bar shows black on the left (0) to white on the right (255). Since you have selected two channels as the target, the Channel pop-up menu displays the abbreviations MY, representing the target channels.

4 Make sure the grayscale bar below the graph shows white on the left to black on the right, causing the input and output densities to be displayed in percentages to match the CMYK values.

5 Click the Load button in the Curves dialog box, and when prompted, choose *Curve02.crv* in *11Project*, and click the Open button.

The Curves dialog box displays the stored settings, and the document window displays the image with no noticeable cast.

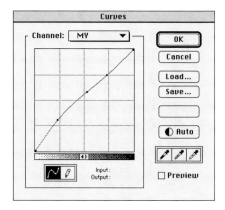

6 In the Curves dialog box click OK.

7 In the Channels palette select the CMYK channel, and save the *11Work.psd* file.

Using the Selective Color command

Adobe Photoshop lets you color correct by using a technique performed by high-end scanners called selective color correction. Selective color correction lets you modify colors by changing the amount of ink used to make a specific color. For example, you can make grass greener by increasing the amount of cyan by 10 percent or remove 5 percent yellow from a red to move the color toward purple.

Note: You must be viewing the composite channel to use the Selective Color command.

1 Choose Adjust from the Image menu and Selective Color from the submenu, and in the Selective Color dialog box make sure the Relative option is selected.

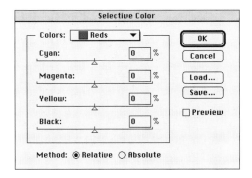

Note: Relative adjusts the existing CMYK values. For example, if you start with 50% magenta and add 10%, 5% is added to the magenta for a total of 55%. Absolute adjusts the color in absolute values. For example, if you start with 50% magenta, the magenta ink is set to a total of 60%.

2 In the Selective Color dialog box choose Reds from the Colors pop-up menu, enter **16** in the Magenta box, and click Preview.

The document window displays too much red in the image.

3 In the Selective Color dialog box enter the following settings:

Cyan .... -10
Magenta.........14
Yellow .... -9
Black 0

4 Click OK to close the Selective Color dialog box.

Applying the Unsharp Mask filter

The Unsharp Mask filter adjusts the contrast of edge detail, creating the illusion of more image sharpness. This filter can be useful for refocusing an image that has become blurry from interpolation or scanning. This filter produces the same effect as the conventional method used to sharpen images on film. In this method, a blurred positive film is sandwiched with a sharp negative file, and the result is shot on high- contrast photographic paper. The filter produces a lighter and darker line on each side of an edge, giving the edge added emphasis.

1 Choose Sharpen from the Filter menu and Unsharp Mask from the submenu.

The Unsharp Mask dialog box prompts you to specify a percentage of the filter's effect, from 1 to 500, in the Amount box. The higher the percentage, the stronger the effect of the filter. You can also indicate the depth of the pixels that will be affected at the edge in the Radius box. The Thresh old option allows you to specify a tolerance range to prevent overall sharpening that might generate noise or cause other unexpected results.

2 In the Unsharp Mask dialog box enter **100%** in the Amount box, **1** pixel in the Radius box, and **9** levels in the Threshold box, and click OK.

The edges of the image are sharpened.

3 Open the *Model.psd* file, and position it so that you can compare the original image with the color corrected *11Work.psd* document.

4 Once you have compared the two files, close the *Model.psd* file.

EDITING THE IMAGE

Now that you have completed color correcting, you will apply the Gaussian Blur along the edge of the model, remove some stray hairs on the model's forehead using the Dust & Scratches filter and the rubber stamp tool, and place the EASTERN STYLE type.

Applying the Gaussian Blur filter

After selecting the green background with the lasso tool, you will feather the selection and apply the Gaussian Blur filter to add a final visual effect.

The Gaussian Blur filter quickly blurs a selection by an adjustable amount. Gaussian refers to the bell-shaped curve that is generated when Adobe Photoshop maps the color values of the affected pixels. This filter can produce a hazy effect.

1 With the lasso tool selected, drag to select the entire background, about one-quarter inch overlapping the model.

Note: Dragging outside of the document window ensures all pixels near the edge of the window are included in the selection.

2 Choose Feather from the Select menu, in the Feather Selection dialog box enter **5** pixels in the Feather Radius box, and click OK.

The edges of the selection are softened.

3 Choose Blur from the Filter menu and Gaussian Blur from the submenu, in the Gaussian Blur dialog box enter **5** pixels in the Radius box, and click OK.

Note: Radius determines the degree of blurring: the higher the value, the stronger the blurring affect.

4 Deselect the background, and save the *11Work.psd* file.

Using the Dust & Scratches filter

You can use the Dust & Scratches filter to remove the individual strands of loose hair on the model's forehead. The Dust and Scratches filter reduces noise in an image by searching the radius of a selection of pixels, allowing you to remove the appearance of irregularities in an image

1 Double-click the lasso tool, and in the Lasso Options palette enter **3** pixels in the Feather box.

2 With the view of the forehead magnified, draw to select the area immediately around a single loose hair on the forehead.

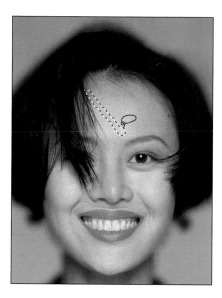

3 Choose Noise from the Filter menu and Dust & Scratches from the submenu, in the Dust & Scratches dialog box enter **2** pixels in the Radius box and **5** levels in the Threshold box, and click OK.

The Radius option determines how far Adobe Photoshop searches to find differing pixels. As you adjust this option, the image gets blurry. Stop when you have the smallest radius which eliminates the defects.

The Threshold option determines how different the value of pixels need to be in order to be eliminated or altered.

Note: Finding the correct compromise between sharpness and concealing the defects may require you to try different combinations of radius and threshold settings. If you can't make the image sharp enough, try reducing the selection area around the defect.

4 Repeat these steps to eliminate a couple more hairs, and then deselect everything.

Using the rubber stamp tool

Use the rubber stamp tool to remove individual hairs on the model's forehead.

1 Click the rubber stamp tool, and in the Brushes palette click the left-most brush in the second row to select a 5-pixel, soft-edged brush.

Note: You may find it useful to press the Caps Lock key to display the cursor as a crosshair.

2 Position the cursor about one-sixteenth of an inch to the right of a hair, hold down the Option key (or Alt key), and click the mouse button.

It may be necessary to take multiple samples near the hair you want to correct, or it may be necessary to select a smaller brush size.

3 Drag along the hair to fill it with the color sampled from the right side of the hair.

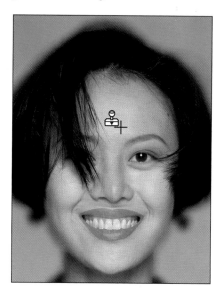

4 Try the same method on a couple more hairs, selecting a new sample point if necessary.

5 Double-click the hand tool to view the entire image, and save the *11Work.psd* file.

Placing the logo box

After placing the white logo box on its own layer (Logo box layer) and adjusting the opacity of the layer to 30%, you will create the logo box's black bar. To add the bar at 100% opacity you will add a new layer, place the black bar, and then merge the layer with the Logo box layer.

1 In the Layers palette click the New Layer icon, in the New Layer dialog box type **Logo box layer** in the Name box, and click OK.

2 Double-click the marquee tool, in the Marquee Options palette make sure Rectangular is selected from the Shape pop-up menu and Fixed Size is selected from the Style pop-up menu, and type **131** pixels in the Width box and **135** pixels in the Height box.

3 Click the document, hold down the mouse button, and drag to position the selection in the upper-left corner of the document, about ¼ inch from the upper and left edges.

4 To fill the logo box with white, choose Fill from the Edit menu, in the Fill dialog box make sure Background Color is selected in the Use pop-up menu, enter **30%** in the Opacity box, and click OK.

5 Deselect the white box.

You will create the logo box's black bar. To add the bar at 100% opacity you will add a new layer, place the black bar, and then merge the layer with the Logo box layer.

6 In the Layers palette click the New Layer icon, in the New Layer dialog box type **Temp layer** in the Name box, and click OK.

7 Double-click the marquee tool, in the Marquee Options palette make sure Rectangular is selected from the Shape pop-up menu, Fixed Size is selected from the Style pop-up menu, and the width is set to 131 pixels, and type **33** pixels in the Height box.

8 With the Temp layer selected in the Layers palette, click over the white logo box in the document window, hold down the mouse button, and drag to position the black bar to be aligned with the top inside edge of the white logo box.

9 Fill the selection with black with an opacity of 100%.

10 Deselect the black bar.

11 In the Layers palette make sure the Temp layer and the Logo box layer are the only layers displayed, and choose Merge Layers from the Layers palette menu.

Both layers are merged into the Logo box layer.

12 Make sure all layers are displayed (eye icons visible).

Placing the type

1 In the Layers palette click the New Layer icon, in the New Layer dialog box type **Type layer** in the Name box, and click OK.

2 With the foreground color set to black, select the type tool, click the white logo box, in the Type Tool dialog box choose Willow from the Font pop-up menu, enter **110** points in the Size box and **2** in the Spacing box, type **STYLE** in uppercase letters in the text box, and click OK.

3 With the edges of the selection hidden, drag to center the type in the white logo box.

4 Make sure the foreground color is set to white.

5 Click the type tool, click the black bar, in the Type Tool dialog box choose Viva 700 Bold 600 Norm from the Font pop-up menu, enter **22** points in the Size box and **2** in the Spacing box, type **EASTERN** in uppercase letters in the text box, and click OK.

6 With the edges of the selection hidden, drag to center the type in the black bar.

7 Deselect the type, and save the *11Work.psd* file.

PRINTING A MAGAZINE COVER

In this example, for the sake of reducing the demand for disk space on your system, you have worked with a file whose dimensions are 5 inches by 7 inches with a resolution of 72 pixels per inch (ppi).

To print a magazine cover, it would be necessary to establish your Adobe Photoshop file size to equal the final printing size. In this case, the dimensions of the magazine cover are meant to be 8¾ inches by 11¼ inches, which allows for a ⅛ inch bleed to produce an 8½ inches by 11 inches cover. To determine the optimal resolution of your working file, you must first know the halftone frequency at which you will be printing. For our purposes, 175 lines per inch (lpi) is satisfactory, and so by doubling the lpi value it is possible to compute the optimal resolution of 350 ppi for our working file resolution. For more information on printing, refer to the *Adobe Photoshop User Guide*.

1 Close all open files, and quit (or exit) the Adobe Photoshop application.

12

Now with layers, you may already recognize the Adobe Photoshop 3.0 application as being the leading multimedia production tool for display screen design. The powerful image editing features combined with the new layering feature pro-

MULTIMEDIA CATALOG

vide tremendous flexibility in creating screens to be incorporated into presentations. ■ For this project, you will create three display screens that are part of an interactive multimedia catalog. With this interactive catalog, a customer can view several colors of the same item by clicking on the corresponding color swatch button. Assembling the necessary components for these screens, you may better appreciate just how much the creative process is streamlined and improved using the Adobe Photoshop application. Also important here is the ability to organize all image information within a single file.

While creating these display screens incorporates techniques found in most of the *Advanced Adobe Photoshop* projects, this project is designed to encompass many of the issues that are specific to designing display screens. For example, since final

MULTIMEDIA CATALOG

output is always displayed in RGB mode with 72 ppi resolution, the files you create should also be in RGB mode with 72 ppi resolution. This project also emphasizes the program's ability to place objects and type, especially desirable here because the images are rasterized for screen display. This project also describes how to use the Save a Copy command to create all three screens from a single Adobe Photoshop file.

The step-by-step instructions in this project cover:

- Resizing the canvas area

- Adding a command to the Commands palette

- Saving and deleting custom colors in the Swatches palette

- Saving a selection to an alpha channel

- Loading stored hue and saturation settings

- Loading a selection from a path

- Using the Save a Copy command.

This project should take about 2 hours to complete.

Viewing the MacroMind demo

Before opening the final file, take a moment to view a demonstration created in the MacroMind Director® software package that features the three display screens you will create.

UNIX platform: The MacroMind Director® demonstration plays on the Macintosh platform or the Windows platform only.

1 Launch the MacroMind Director demonstration.

Macintosh platform: Double-click the Interactive Catalog *icon in the* CATALOG *folder on the* Advanced Adobe Photoshop *CD-ROM disc to launch the MacroMind Director demonstration.*

Windows platform: Open the catalog.exe *file in the root directory on the* Advanced Adobe Photoshop *CD-ROM disc to launch the MacroMind Director demonstration.*

2 Click the color swatches in the lower-right corner of the screen to view the three colors.

3 Quit the demonstration.

Macintosh platform: Hold down the Command key and press period (.) to quit the demo.

Windows platform: Press the Esc key to quit the demo.

Viewing the final image

It may seem that the MacroMind Director demonstration uses a single screen, changing the blouse color only. In fact, this demonstration consists of three separate screens. Rather than saving three separate files, the *12Final.psd* file contains all the image information for all three screens.

1 Before launching the Adobe Photoshop application, throw away the Adobe Photoshop Preferences file to ensure all settings are returned to their default values.

2 Launch the Adobe Photoshop application, and open the *12Final.psd* file in *12Project* to view the final image of this document.

The Layers palette for the *12Final.psd* document includes two layers, containing the two additional blouse colors.

3 Experiment by hiding and showing the layers to view the results.

4 Select the full screen without menu bar icon in the bottom-right corner of the toolbox to view the image as it appears as the demonstration screen.

Note: Press the Tab key to hide the toolbox, and then press the Tab key to show the toolbox.

5 Click the standard window icon in the bottom-left corner of the toolbox to view the image in the standard window.

6 Reduce the view of the *12Final.psd* document, and drag it to the upper-right corner of your desktop to use as a visual reference.

CREATING A DOCUMENT

After opening an existing Adobe Photoshop file, you will add work canvas area, and rename the document. Since the purpose of this project is to create display screens, it is best to edit the document in RGB mode.

Resizing the work canvas

The Canvas Size command allows you to add work space, or extra work canvas area, around an image without changing the dimensions of the image. If you use the Canvas Size command to crop an image, you might lose image information you cannot recover.

Note: Use the Image Size command or the cropping tool to adjust the size or resolution of an image.

1 Open the *Photo.psd file* in *12Project*.

2 Choose Canvas Size from the Image menu, in the Canvas Size dialog box enter **640** pixels in the Width box, make sure the Height equals 480 pixels, click the center-left square of the Placement box (to position the image in the center-left portion of the canvas), and click OK.

Since this document consists of a Background layer, the document window displays the image to the left of the default white background.

Note: 680 pixels by 480 pixels is the full frame size for a 13-inch monitor.

3 Save the *Photo.psd* file as *12Work.psd* to *Projects*.

Customizing the Commands palette

Since the Float command is used frequently in this project, you will customize the Commands palette to include it.

1 In the Commands palette choose New Command from the Command palette menu, in the New Command dialog box type **Float** in the Name box, select F10 (an unassigned function key) from the Function Key pop-up menu, select a color from the Color pop-up menu, and click OK.

The Commands palette displays the newly assigned function key.

Creating the black vertical bar

1 Double-click the marquee tool, in the Marquee Options palette choose Rectangular from the Shape pop-up menu, choose Fixed Size from the Style menu, and enter **16** pixels in the Width box and **480** pixels in the Height box.

2 Click the document window to create a selection, and fill the selection with black.

3 Drag the selection until its left edge is flush with the right edge of the photo as shown in the illustration below.

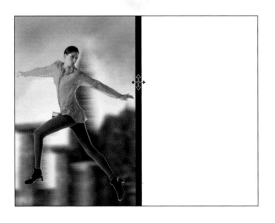

Creating the COLORS box

1 In the Marquee Options palette enter **105** pixels in the Width box and **250** pixels in the Height box.

2 Click the document to create a selection, and fill the selection with black.

3 Drag it to the lower-right corner of the window.

Creating the light blue box

1 In the Marquee Options palette enter **140** pixels in the Width box and **20** pixels in the Height box.

2 Click the document to create the selection.

3 Click the foreground color control in the toolbox, and in the Color Picker dialog box enter the following settings:

Red 163
Green........... 187
Blue 222

4 Click OK to set the foreground color to light blue.

5 Fill the rectangle with the light blue color.

6 With the edges of the selection hidden, drag it just above the color swatch box.

SAVING A CUSTOM COLOR

Just to show you how easy it is to save a custom color, we've included the next few steps where you will save the light blue color (you just selected) in the Swatches palette.

1 With the Swatches palette open, position the cursor over an empty space in the bottom of the Swatches palette so that it is displayed as the paint bucket tool, and click to add the light blue color.

2 Click the empty space again to add the same color twice.

3 To delete the newly added swatch from the Swatches palette, hold down the Command key (or Ctrl key) and position the cursor over the swatch so that it is displayed as a scissors tool, and click to delete it.

4 Experiment with deleting any number of existing swatches to see how the remaining swatches move left to eliminate an emptied square in a swatch row.

5 To return to the default Swatches palette, choose Reset Swatches from the Swatches palette menu, and when prompted, click OK.

Stroking the light blue box

The next steps will fill a black border around the light blue box.

1 Click the default colors icon in the toolbox to set the foreground color to black.

2 With the light blue box still selected, choose Stroke from the Edit menu, in the Stroke dialog box type **2** pixels in the Width box and select the Center button, type **100**% in the Opacity box, choose Normal from the Mode pop-up menu, and click OK.

Creating the yellow box

1 In the Marquee Options palette enter **280** pixels in the Width box and **90** pixels in the Height box.

2 Click the document window, and drag to position the selection about 1 inch below the top of the work canvas, with its left edge overlapping the photographic image by about 1 inch.

3 In the Picker palette drag the sliders to the following settings:

    Red 240
    Green 236
    Blue 168

4 Choose Fill from the Edit menu, in the Fill dialog box make sure Foreground Color is selected from the Use pop-up menu, enter **60%** in the Opacity box, and click OK.

5 Deselect the box, and save the *12Work.psd* file.

Drawing the black vertical line

It may be necessary to zoom once in the *12Final.psd* image to view this vertical line in the upper-right portion of the window.

1 Choose Show Rulers from the Window menu to display the rulers.

By default, the units on the rulers are marked by inches.

2 Choose Preferences from the File menu and Units from the submenu, in the Unit Preferences dialog box choose Pixels from the Ruler Units pop-up menu, and click OK.

3 With the foreground color set to black, double-click the line tool, and in the Line Tool Options palette enter **2** pixels in the Line Width box.

4 Make sure the Info palette is open, so that you can view the coordinates of the cursor's position in the document.

5 To draw the line, position the cursor at the top of the light blue box, aligned with top ruler mark 535 pixels, click the document window, hold down the Shift key (to constrain the angle of the line to 45°), drag up to the top of the window, and release the mouse button.

Creating the black ellipse

1 In the Marquee Options palette, choose Elliptical from the Shape pop-up menu, and type **200** pixels in the Width box and type **42** pixels in the Height box.

2 With the move tool selected, drag the ellipse to position it in the upper-right corner of the window, evenly centered between the top of the window and the yellow box.

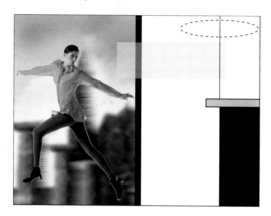

3 Fill the selection with black with an opacity of 100%, and deselect it.

Creating the small black boxes

1 In the Marquee Options palette choose Rectangular from the Shape pop-up menu, and enter **95** pixels in the Width box and **25** pixels in the Height box.

2 Click the document, and drag the selection until the crosshair in the upper-left corner of the selection is aligned approximately with top ruler mark 360 pixels and left ruler mark 235 pixels.

3 Fill the selection with black.

4 Click the document, and drag the selection until the crosshair in the upper-left corner of the selection is aligned approximately with top ruler mark 360 pixels and left ruler mark 350 pixels.

5 Fill the selection with black.

6 Deselect the rectangle.

Drawing the pointing lines

The small black boxes have lines that point to the blouse and pants in the photographic image.

1 Double-click the line tool, and in the Line Tool Options palette make sure the line width is set to 2 pixels.

2 Click the upper-left corner of the lower small box, hold down the Shift key, drag to the back leg of the woman, and release the mouse button to draw the line that points to the pants.

3 With the line tool selected, click the upper-left corner of the upper small box, hold down the Shift key, drag left to the blouse, and release the mouse button to draw the line that points to the blouse

4 Save the *12Work.psd* file.

PLACING THE TYPE

As a rule of thumb, you maintain a great deal of flexibility in your design whenever you place type on a layer of its own.

Placing the COLORS type

1 In the Layers palette click the New Layer icon, in the New Layer dialog box type **Type layer** in the Name box, and click OK.

2 In the Picker palette drag the sliders to the following settings:

Red 50
Green 70
Blue 70

3 Select the type tool, click the large black box in the lower-right corner, in the Type Tool dialog box choose Palatino™ Roman from the Font pop-up menu, enter **55** points in the Size box, type **COLORS** in uppercase letters in the text box, and click OK.

4 Choose Rotate from the Image menu and 90° CCW (counterclockwise) from the submenu to rotate the selection.

5 With the move tool selected, drag in the document window to position the type about ¼ inch from the right side of the large black box, centered between the top and bottom of the box.

6 Deselect the type.

Placing the mix & match type

1 Set the foreground color to black.

2 Select the type tool, click the light blue box above the COLORS box, in the Type Tool dialog box choose Courier Regular from the Font pop-up menu, enter **20** in the Size box, type **mix & match** in lowercase letters in the text box, and click OK.

3 With the edges of the selection hidden, use the arrow keys to position the type to be centered in the light blue box.

4 Deselect the type.

Placing the Jump into fall fashions type

1 In the Layers palette make sure the Type layer is selected.

2 Select the type tool, click the yellow box, in the Type Tool dialog box choose Palatino Roman from the Font pop-up menu, enter **40** in the Size box, enter **42** in the Leading box, in the text box type **Jump into**, press the Return key (or Enter key), and then type **fall fashions!**, and click OK.

3 With the edges of the selection hidden, use the arrow keys to position the type to be centered in the yellow box.

4 Deselect the type.

Placing the INTERACTIVE type

1 Set the foreground color to white.

2 In the Layers palette make sure the Type layer is selected.

3 Select the type tool, click the ellipse in the upper-right corner of the window, in the Type Tool dialog box choose Courier Bold from the Font pop-up menu, enter **13** in the Size box, type **0** in the Leading box, enter **5** in the Spacing box, type **INTERACTIVE** in uppercase letters in the text box, and click OK.

4 With the edges of the selection hidden, use the arrow keys to position the type in the upper-left portion of the ellipse.

5 Deselect the type, and save the *12Work.psd* file.

Creating the small yellow box

Assuming the Type layer is exclusively for type, you will select the Background layer to be the target layer before positioning the small yellow box in the black ellipse.

1 In the Layers palette select the Background layer.

2 In the Marquee Options palette enter **66** pixels in the Width box and **12** pixels in the Height box.

3 Click the document, and drag to position the selection in the ellipse under the INTERACTIVE type with its left edge aligned with the black hairline as shown in the illustration below.

4 Select the eyedropper tool, and click the existing yellow box to sample the yellow color.

5 Choose Fill from the Edit menu, in the Fill dialog box type **100%** in the Opacity box, and click OK.

6 Deselect the rectangle.

Placing the catalog type

1 In the Layers palette select the Type layer.

2 Set the foreground color to black.

3 Select the type tool, click the small yellow box, in the Type Tool dialog box choose Helvetica Bold from the Font pop-up menu, enter **13** points in the Size box, enter **2** in the Spacing box, type **catalog** in lowercase letters in the text box, and click OK.

4 With the edges of the selection hidden, use the arrow keys to position the type to be centered in the small yellow box.

5 Deselect the type.

Placing the Blouse type

1 Set the foreground color to white.

2 Select the type tool, click the upper small box, in the Type Tool dialog box make sure Helvetica Bold is selected from the Font pop-up menu, type **24** points in the Size box, enter **0** in the Spacing box, type **Blouse** in the text box, and click OK.

3 With the edges of the selection hidden, use the arrow keys to position the type in the lower-left corner of the upper small box.

4 Deselect the type.

Placing the Pants type

1 In the Layers palette make sure the Type layer is selected.

2 Make sure the foreground color is set to white.

3 Select the type tool, click the lower small box, in the Type Tool dialog box make sure Helvetica Bold is selected from the Font pop-up menu, make sure the size equals 24 points, type **Pants** in the text box, and click OK.

4 With the edges of the selection hidden, use the arrow keys to position the type to the upper-right corner of the lower small black box.

5 Deselect the type.

Placing the prices type

1 In the Layers palette make sure the Type layer is selected.

2 In the Picker palette drag the sliders to the following settings:

    Red 166
    Green 172
    Blue 145

3 Select the type tool, click just below the Blouse box, in the Type Tool dialog box choose Palatino Roman from the Font pop-up menu, enter **55** points in the Size box, type **$147** in the text box, and click OK.

4 With the edges of the selection hidden, use the arrow keys to position the type so that the top edge of the type is flush with the bottom edge of the Blouse box, aligning the "4" with the right edge of the Blouse box.

5 Deselect the type.

6 Select the type tool, click just below the Pants box, in the Type Tool dialog box type **$98** in the text box, and click OK.

7 With the edges of the selection hidden, use the arrow keys to position the type so that the top edge of the type is flush with the bottom edge of the Pants box, aligning the "9" with the right edge of the Pants box.

8 Deselect the type, and save the *12Work.psd* file.

CREATING THE COLOR SWATCHES

You will position and colorize three color swatches in the Colors box in the lower-right corner of the window.

1 In the Layers palette select the Background layer to be the target.

2 In the Marquee Options palette enter **46** pixels in the Width box and **36** pixels in the Height box.

3 In the document window drag to position the rectangle selection over the blouse as shown in the illustration below.

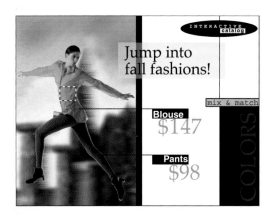

4 Hold down the Option key (or Alt key) and drag in the document window to position the selection in the Colors box, aligning the left edge of the selection with the left edge of the Colors box, about ¾ inch below the light blue box as shown in the illustration below.

5 Choose Save Selection from the Select menu, and in the Save Selection dialog box click OK.

The selection is saved in an alpha channel.

6 Hold down the Option key (or Alt key) and the Shift key (to constrain the movement to 45°) and drag down from the first color swatch to position the duplicate swatch about ½ inch below the first swatch.

7 Choose Adjust from the Image menu and Hue/Saturation from the submenu, and click Load in the Hue/Saturation dialog box.

8 When prompted, select the *12SetA.hss* file in *12Project*, and click Open.

9 In the Hue/Saturation dialog box click OK to apply the color correction settings to adjust the color of the second swatch from tangerine to violet.

To duplicate the top swatch once more, you will load the selection previously saved to the alpha channel to select the top swatch.

Note: For this exercise, it is important to duplicate the tangerine-colored swatch twice, since adjustments to hue and saturation of both duplicate color swatches are relative to the tangerine-colored swatch.

10 Choose Load Selection from the Select menu, in the Load Selection dialog box make sure channel #4 is selected in the Channel pop-up menu, and click OK to select the top swatch.

11 Hold down the Option key (or Alt key) and the Shift key (to constrain the movement to 45°) and drag down from the top color swatch to position the third swatch about ½ inch below the second swatch.

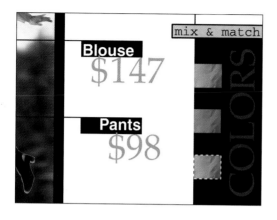

12 Choose Adjust from the Image menu and Hue/Saturation from the submenu, and click Load in the Hue/Saturation dialog box.

13 When prompted, select the *12SetB.hss* file in *12Project*, and click Open.

14 In the Hue/Saturation dialog box click OK to apply the color correction settings to adjust the color of the third swatch from tangerine to rose.

15 Deselect the swatch, and save the *12Work.psd* file.

LOADING A SELECTION STORED AS A PATH

Before adjusting the hue and saturation of the blouse, you will select the blouse by loading a selection stored as a path that exists in the *12Work.psd* file. This path had been saved previously in the *Photo.psd file* that you opened and renamed *12Work.psd.*

1 With the Background layer still selected in the Layers palette, open the Paths palette, and make sure the Blouse path is selected.

2 In the Paths palette choose Make Selection from the Paths palette menu, in the Make Selection dialog box type **1** pixel in the Feather box (to smooth the edges of the selection), and click OK.

Colorizing the blouse image

Rather than creating three separate Adobe Photoshop files, it is possible to contain all the image information for the three screens in one file. For this reason you will create two new layers, containing the two additional blouse colors.

1 With the blouse still selected, float the selection.

2 In the Layers palette double-click the Floating Selection, in the Make Layer dialog box type **Violet blouse layer** in the Name box, and click OK.

The Layers palette displays the Violet blouse layer above the Background layer.

3 In the Layers palette drag the Violet blouse layer to the New Layer icon.

4 Double-click the Violet blouse layer copy in the Layers palette, in the Layer Options dialog box, type **Rose blouse layer** in the Name box, and click OK.

The Layers palette displays the Rose blouse layer above the Violet blouse layer.

5 With the Rose blouse layer selected in the Layers palette, choose Adjust from the Image menu and Hue/Saturation from the submenu, and in the Hue/Saturation dialog box click Load.

6 When prompted, select the *12SetB.hss* file in *12Project*, and click Open.

7 In the Hue/Saturation dialog box click OK to apply the color correction settings to adjust the color of the blouse from tangerine to rose.

WINDOWS PLATFORM:

RENAME ALL *.HSS

FILES TO *.AHU.

RENAME ALL *.CRV

FILES TO *.ACV.

8 Hide the Rose blouse layer.

9 With the Violet blouse layer selected in the Layers palette, choose Adjust from the Image menu and Hue/Saturation from the submenu, and in the Hue/Saturation dialog box click Load.

10 When prompted, select the *12SetA.hss* file in *12Project*, and click Open.

11 In the Hue/Saturation dialog box click OK to apply the color correction settings to adjust the color of the blouse from tangerine to violet.

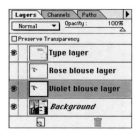

12 Deselect the blouse image, and view the results of hiding and showing various layers,

In this example, the display of the Type layer is not affected by the addition of the Violet blouse layer or the Rose blouse layer because the blouse image does not overlap any of the type.

13 Save the *12Work.psd* file.

USING THE SAVE A COPY COMMAND

The Save a Copy command lets you save a copy of a file without replacing or affecting the current open file you are working in. When you use the Save a Copy command you specify how to save the file: with all its channels and layers intact; or as a flattened version of the file, where all visible layers have been merged.

Saving a flattened copy

As was said before, it is necessary to create three separate screens for this interactive catalog. Each of these files must be flattened to be exported from Adobe Photoshop.

When you use the Save a Copy command with the desired layers visible for each screen and with the Flatten image option selected, the current (open) file remains intact, allowing you to save three flattened versions of the current file *12Work.psd*.

1 In the Layers palette make sure all layers are displayed (eye icons visible), except for Rose blouse layer and Violet blouse layer, and choose Save a Copy from the File menu.

Note: Any layers that are not displayed will not be included in the saved, flattened version.

2 When prompted, make sure *Projects* is selected in the pop-up menu, type **12FlatA.psd** in the Name box, click the Flatten Image option, and click Save (or OK).

The layers are now merged into the Background layer for the *12FlatA.psd* file.

Note: When you use the Save a Copy command, the current open file remains intact.

3 Repeat the previous two steps, making sure the Violet blouse layer is displayed (eye icon visible) and Rose blouse layer is hidden, and naming the flattened file *12FileB.psd* to create the display screen that displays the violet-colored blouse.

4 Again, repeat the first two steps, making sure the Rose blouse layer is displayed (eye icon visible), and naming the flattened file *12FileC.psd* to create the display screen that displays the rose-colored blouse.

Once you have exported the files to the Macro-Mind Director application or to another presentation software package, you may wish to delete all flattened images, retaining only the *12Work.psd* file.

5 Close all open files, and quit (or exit) the Adobe Photoshop application.

INDEX

COLOPHON

DOCUMENTATION

Author: Robin Krueger

Editors: Robin Krueger, Kisa Harris

Project Designer: Andrew Faulkner, Andrew Faulkner Design

Art Director: Sharon Anderson

Illustrator: Jeffrey Schaaf

Book Production: Jeffrey Schaaf

Book Production Management: Kisa Harris

Publication Management: Kisa Harris

Photographs: Stan Musilek (Projects 2-12), Leslie Hirsch (Project 1)

Cover and Book Design: Sharon Anderson

Cover Illustration: John Ritter

Cover Photography: Scott Peterson, Sharon Anderson, John Ritter

Adobe Teach Movies: Andrew Faulkner, Robin Krueger, Neil Passero, Jeffrey Schaaf

Film Production: Cheryl Elder, Karen Winguth

Scanning: The Typemasters, Palo Alto, CA

Legal Advisor: Paul Klein™

Adobe Press: Patrick Ames

Special thanks to: Rita Amladi, Patrice Anderson, Fred Barling, Matt Brown, Russell Brown, John Doughty, Necia Doughty, Jon Ferraiolo, Jerry Granucci, George Jardine, Carita Klevickis, Bryan Lamkin, John Leddy, Kate O'Day, Mary Anne Petrillo, Glen Pierre, Gloria Robles, Sarah Rosenbaum, Nora Sandoval, Eric Thomas

Alpha Test-Teach Participants:
Rita Amladi, Adobe Technical Support
Matt Brown, Adobe Technical Support
Laura Dower, Adobe Technical Publications
Kim Isola, Adobe Technical Publications
Kisa Harris, Adobe Training Manager
Robin Krueger, Adobe Educational Services

Beta Test-Teach Participants:
Rita Amladi, Adobe Technical Support
Angela Anderson, Adobe Technical Sales Support
Patrice Anderson, Adobe Educational Services
Sharon Anderson, Adobe Educational Services
Matt Brown, Adobe Technical Support
John Doughty, Adobe Educational Services
Mikyong Han, Adobe Special Projects
Kisa Harris, Adobe Training Manager
Ingrid Hung, Adobe Special Projects
Lisa Jeans, Adobe Special Projects
Robin Krueger, Adobe Educational Services
Bobbi Long, Designer/Instructor
John Lund, Photographer
Liz Ryan, Designer

PRODUCTION NOTES

This book was created electronically using FrameMaker® on the Macintosh Quadra® 800. Art was produced using Adobe Illustrator, Adobe Photoshop, and SnapJot™ on the Macintosh Quadra 800. Working film was produced with the PostScript language on an Agfa® 5000 Imagesetter. The Frutiger™ and Minion families of typefaces are used throughout this book.

Adobe Training Resources

The Classroom in a Book™ series, a set of intermediate and advanced workbooks, guides you through many step-by-step lessons to help you learn to master the powerful features of Adobe's products. The series is available for Adobe Illustrator,™ Adobe Photoshop™ and Adobe Premiere.™

If finding time to focus is difficult, or if you think an instructor-led training program will augment your learning curve, investigate some of the many professional training businesses or educational institutions using this very same Classroom in a Book. Instructors can provide feedback and guidance that go beyond the contents of this book in a classroom setting.

For training referral suggestions in North America, call:
Adobe's Customer Services at 1-800-833-6687.
In Europe and the Pacific Rim, call your local distributor.